Contents

Foreword

This book is a memorial to its author and only begetter, Don Crompton, who died before completing it. It was written not as a celebration of the resurgence of interest in Golding's work in the last few years, but as a labour of love and the outcome of many years' thought. From the first Don had greatly admired Golding's novels and wanted to share his pleasure and insights with others. In Spring 1967 he published his interpretation of *The Spire* in the *Critical Quarterly*, in part as a response to that book's doubtful or adverse critical reception. He resumed work on Golding after the appearance of *Darkness Visible* in 1979, fascinated by its visionary quality and eager to unravel the significance of its frequent biblical allusions. His account of these appeared in *Twentieth Century Literature* (Summer 1982), in an issue devoted to Golding's recent work. The present book now began to take shape, with the addition of chapters on *The Pyramid* and *Rites of Passage*, and a long introductory analysis of those poetic elements that Don felt to be characteristic of Golding's later phase. Its completion was prevented by illness and his death in September 1983.

Don Crompton's approach to Golding, though professional in the best sense, was not that of the professional critic, but of the teacher, keen to communicate his enthusiasm to students who found the novels less accessible than he did. His admiration sprang from a deep sympathy with the novelist's outlook: in Golding's 'universal pessimism and cosmic optimism', his sense of life as dark, complex and mysterious, yet illuminated by moments of joy and affirmation, and in his passionately held yet tentative religious convictions, Don found his inmost feelings reflected. As men of the same generation, they had inevitably lived through the same events and perhaps drawn similar conclusions from them: although ten years younger, Don's early life, like Golding's, was largely shaped by his war experiences, first in the Middle East, then in the Far East. On his return he took a first in English at Manchester University and became a schoolmaster, and then a lecturer at Didsbury College of Education. Here he was rapidly promoted to Head of English, and passed on his own involvement to a generation of young teachers. In 1969 he was appointed Principal of Westminster College, the college of education on the outskirts of Oxford. It was here that I first met Don in the early 1970s, and was immediately struck by his warmth and forceful personality – he didn't seem to have been smoothed into the characterless administration man that one normally encounters in such posts. A man of exceptional energy, intelligence and integrity, he was full of first-hand responses to everything that came his way, as if time had never dulled the freshness of experience for him. That fresh eye for experience was one of the qualities he valued in Golding.

In preparing Don's manuscript for publication, I am uneasily aware of having exceeded my editorial brief; I could not resist expanding or developing a number of points which seemed to hold out promising lines of thought. Nearly all such additions have been prompted by ideas, suggestions, sometimes particular words used in Don's original text, but in the opening and closing paragraphs of chapters I have allowed myself to indulge in speculations which it may be that Don, with a greater regard for justice and temperance, might not have endorsed. The chapters on *The Scorpion God* and *The Paper Men* have been added at the request of the publisher.

Finally I would like to acknowledge the several kinds of help I have received: Craig Raine kindly lent me the tape of his radio programme on Golding, *Cabin'd, Cribb'd, Confin'd*, broadcast on 23 December 1983; John Bodley of Faber and Faber provided me with some cuttings of interviews; Dr Helen Whitehouse of the Ashmolean answered questions about Egyptology; Humaira Ahmed typed much of the manuscript, at great speed, and my husband Robin has helped and listened throughout. I particularly want to thank Mary Crompton, and Sarah and Simon; they searched out notes and missing references, sent cuttings, and patiently criticised and discussed my alterations to the text at every stage. Had Don lived to see his book through the press, I believe it would have been dedicated to them.

Julia Briggs
Hertford College

Acknowledgements

The publisher and the editor would like to express their thanks for permission to include extracts as follows: passages reprinted by permission of Faber and Faber Ltd from *The Spire, Darkness Visible, Rites of Passage* and *The Paper Men* by William Golding; excerpts reprinted by permission of Farrar, Straus and Giroux, Inc., from *Darkness Visible* © 1979 by William Golding, *Rites of Passage* © 1980 by William Golding, *The Paper Men* © 1984 by William Golding; excerpts from *The Spire,* © 1964 by William Golding, reprinted by permission of Harcourt, Brace, Jovanovich, Inc.

The Department of Antiquities at the Ashmolean Museum, Oxford, kindly gave permission to reproduce the mace-head figure shown on p. 81.

Introduction

It seems to me to be a perfectly normal function of
writing to see what is happening; the film is, at it were,
unwinding before your eyes, life is going on and one is
like an American spy satellite, one can swoop and . . .
bring one's camera down until you can read Pravda in
large print from two hundred miles up.

William Golding

We'll . . . take upon's the mystery of things
As if we were God's spies.

King Lear, V.iii. 16-7

'It was so simple at first . . . I had a vision you see, a clear and
explicit vision. It was *so* simple! It was to be my work. I was
chosen for it. But then the complications began.' The speaker
is Jocelin in *The Spire*, Golding's fifth novel and one so different
in its attitude to experience from the preceding four that it
may be called the first book of his later phase. For until *The
Spire*, Golding's novels had been structured along dialectical
lines: in *Lord of the Flies* there is a struggle between reason and
the savagery that springs from terror; in *The Inheritors* it takes

place between the prelapsarian Neanderthal people and our fallen, intelligent ancestors; in *Pincher Martin* between Pincher's will to live and the providence beyond him; in *Free Fall* between Sammy innocent and free and Sammy the prisoner of what he has done. In each of these the issues are complex but clear cut, and the author's view of the moral significance of the action is never in doubt. His role is judicial, almost omniscient, and as a result these novels lie open to exposition, anatomically compact and well-formed, for each attains a level of technical perfection that Golding was not to achieve, nor even to strive for, again. They are books written out of dark and unhesitating convictions, about 'the end of innocence, the darkness of man's heart'. Only in the last of them, *Free Fall*, with Sammy's uncovenanted vision after the nightmare of the cell, does the work begin to open out towards the inexplicable and mysterious connections between horror and glory. In *The Spire* Jocelin's final unmouthed questions – 'What is terror and joy, how should they be mixed, why are they the same, the flashing, the flying through the panicshot darkness like a bluebird over water?' – pass beyond the defined areas of conflict of the earlier books, and open a way to the fruitful uncertainties, mysteries, doubts of Golding's later work.

Inevitably there are many points of continuity between the first four novels and *The Spire:* men possessed by primitive terror sacrifice the alien to the unknown, guilt and innocence remain primary forces, and – as in *Pincher Martin* and *Free Fall* – the flashbacks work as cumulative indictments of the relentlessly gripping will that refuses to see anything but its determined end. As in *The Inheritors* (and the more recent *Rites of Passage*), *The Spire*'s graphic recreation of history arose from a question Golding put to himself: how did the 400 foot spire of Salisbury cathedral come to be built, using only the simplest of constructional principles and the labour of men's hands? Yet it remains a profoundly different novel from its predecessors in that there is a mystery about the moral significance of the central event; is Jocelin's edifice inspired by faith, saintly folly, demonic will, repressed sexuality or even all at once? 'My spire pierced every stage, from the bottom to the top', he tries to explain to Father Adam. There is more than a hint that Jocelin's visions of the kingfisher and the blossoming apple tree hold opposed experiences of terror and joy in synthesis, recalling the tree of the knowledge of good and evil, forces that 'as two twins cleaving together leapt forth into the world', in Milton's phrase. To the dying Jocelin, good and evil appear inextricably intertwined; the beauty of the spire and the apple tree are deeply rooted in human pain and guilt. Golding has here exchanged a controlling and determining knowledge for a sense of the overwhelming mystery inherent in the creation of any great work of art: in Jocelin's words, 'God knows where God may be', and 'Now – I know nothing at all.'

A sense of cosmic significance, of something that seemed almost to speak from behind or beyond the novelist himself, had been present intermittently in earlier books, in the voices that spoke to Simon and Pincher, the vision that came to Sammy, but in *The Spire* it had arrived at the centre of the novel. Golding has recently said that the quality he was concerned with in this novel 'was how a mystery presented itself to me and raised the question of how far a novelist knows what he is writing'.[1] It is no accident that as the artist abandoned his position of certainty, he stepped, in the nakedness of his dilemmas, into his own book. *The Spire* is about the inextricable mixture of faith, folly, arrogance and sublimated desire that makes every work of art at once a miracle and a self-betrayal. It is about the artist's blind plunge into the pit that is his own subconscious mind, and about the terrible cost of that plunge.

The Spire marked a watershed in Golding's career in a number of ways. In considering the sources and nature of the change that took place in his work, it is instructive to look back at Golding's reputation as it stood in 1964 when the book was about to appear. It was certainly one of the most eagerly awaited books of the decade. The immediate post-war years, as George Orwell had forecast in 'Inside the Whale', were not a good time for the creative artist to be at work. Among the writers to emerge since 1946, William Golding was regarded as exceptional, a novelist with something new and exciting to say. His first novel *Lord of the Flies* had been a huge success on both sides of the Atlantic, as, in a quieter way, *The Inheritors* had been. But there were some reservations expressed about *Pincher Martin*, and *Free Fall* occasioned more. Nevertheless there was still a feeling that if any post-war novelist would write the novel that would live for its time, as books like *A Passage to India*, *Ulysses* or *The Rainbow* had lived for theirs, that novelist would be William Golding.

A sense of expectation was intensified by the increased time gap between the novels. *Lord of the Flies*, *The Inheritors* and *Pincher Martin* had all been published at yearly intervals from 1954 to 1956. *Free Fall* had interrupted this pattern by appearing three years later; and now a still longer gap separated that book from *The Spire*. The significance of the greater time lag between the novels was intriguing. When *Free Fall* was published in 1959, it was generally understood (and Golding himself gave some support to the view) that the delay was largely due to the book's greater complexity, to the more intense and prolonged wrestling that results when a writer no longer sees the problems of experience as susceptible to simple solutions, but recognises them as endlessly proliferating, paradoxical, and intractable.

Free Fall itself clearly reflected the effect of this struggle. Apparently abandoning the meticulous planning, the well-organised division and sub-division, the firmly controlled point of view which had characterised his earlier books, Golding seemed to be experimenting, letting the work run free in quite a new way, no longer certain as to where it was taking him. By 1962, three years after the publication of *Free Fall*, Golding was ready to speak of the way in which his attitude to his work had changed since *Lord of the Flies:* in a lecture given to the students of UCLA he explained:[2]

I no longer believe that the author has a sort of *patria potestas* over his brainchildren. Once they are printed they have reached their majority and the author has no more authority over them, knows no more about them, perhaps knows less about them than the critic who comes fresh to them, and sees them not as the author hoped they would be, but as what they are.

This change of mind partly reflected the impact of different critical interpretations of his work on the novelist, but it also suggested that Golding's concept of his own shaping intention was beginning to loosen. The structure of *Free Fall* felt more improvised than the earlier novels had done, and the book met with some hostility from the critics on publication. Golding seemed prepared to allow they might be right when, in an interview, he described it as 'a confession of growth or a confession of failure'.[3] Twenty years later, he treated its reception more sceptically, and when James Baker commented in an interview that '*Free Fall* was a novel that irritated a lot of readers and critics . . . because of its peculiar structure', Golding replied 'Good, good, good . . . splendid.'[4]

The critical consensus seemed to be that *Free Fall* had many fine individual passages and was as ever commendably ambitious in scope, but it just did not achieve the artistic coherence that the earlier novels had done. And nowhere was this more obvious than in the style, which by post-war utility standards often seemed heavily mannered, over-inflated, self-conscious and self-indulgent in a way that was difficult to accept. In *The Inheritors* Golding had been faced with the enormous task of recreating awareness in creatures for whom no recognised language existed, and he had managed it with an incomparable display of imaginative and linguistic inventiveness. *Pincher Martin* had also used language with great audacity, shifting gear from highly colloquial and slangy dialogue to passages of visionary poetic intensity. After experiments of this kind, it was hardly likely that Golding would revert to the more conventional style of his first book, even though *Free Fall* was concerned with times, places and people that at first sight seemed considerably more familiar, since it told the story of a child growing up in England between the wars.

Each of Golding's first three books had made use of other books to 'kick off' from (Ballantyne's *Coral Island*, H.G. Wells's *The Grisly Folk*, Taffrail's *Pincher Martin OD*). *Free Fall* had no such specific starting-point, though in significant ways it drew upon the tradition of the *Bildungsroman*, the novel of the artist growing up in society, and on one example of the form in particular, James Joyce's *Portrait of the Artist as a Young Man*. Golding's attitude to Joyce seems to be one of reluctant admiration; morally and temperamentally they are deeply at odds and yet they both set themselves comparable artistic goals. As a model, Joyce's *Portrait of the Artist* focuses determinedly and self-consciously on the language that is its medium; indeed the whole progress of Stephen Dedalus from babyhood to youth is depicted linguistically, from the earliest of baby noises to philosophical debates on the relative nature of language. Throughout, the character of language itself and the human process of acquiring and mastering it is held up for inspection. *Free Fall* makes no comparable enquiry into its own constituent elements, but is concerned instead to make exactly the kind of moral discriminations that Joyce had deliberately refused to endorse; even so Golding's brilliant recreation of childhood from the inside seems consciously to invite comparison with the earlier masterpiece and in doing so, focuses, as Joyce had done, on sound effects. For Joyce's short-sighted hero, noises – a train going in and out of tunnels, the whistles and keys of the guards, the sound of cricket bats ('pick, pack, pock, puck') recreate the fresh, sensuous response of the child to its incomprehensible environment. Golding uses comparable effects, notably in the scene where the child Sammy accepts his friend Philip's dare to defile the local church by urinating on the altar. The children's terror is conveyed by a kind of shorthand – 'Giggle flap tremor, heart-thud' – while the soft opening and closing of the church door becomes the sinister 'wuff . . . wubb wuff' before Sammy's eardrum explodes, as the Verger cuffs him.

Extravagantly vivid metaphors convey the inexperienced and puzzling perceptions of childhood. Teachers seem as endlessly tall and distant as trees, even when they too are comically threatened by a higher authority:

> There came a time when we sensed that the trees were tossed by a high wind. There was to be an inspection and the trees whispered the news down to us. A taller tree was coming to find out if we were happy and good and learning things.

Sammy's role as an artist and by extension a poet encouraged Golding to take startling liberties with his reader. He deliberately drew attention to Sammy's translation of experience into graphic terms, to his self-conscious and stylised self-presentation, and further, to his visual awareness of the way words reach the reader. Joyce's emphasis on language is thus exchanged for a closer focus on the text itself, the peculiar mode by which the writer communicates with his reader:

> I am poised eighteen inches over the black rivets you are reading.

> I see her voice, a jagged shape of scarlet and bronze, shatter the air.

> I saw the very water of sorrow hanging honey-thick in eyelashes or dashed down a cheek like an exclamation mark at the beginning of a Spanish sentence.

Devices of this kind now seem effectively unconventional, but initially they were regarded with suspicion, as gratuitous affectations on Golding's part. The book's linguistic range included the slang of the playground and the slums alongside the pretentiously literary language of adolescent passion. Its subject matter extended to an intense, often painful and always realistic appreciation of the body's wayward and sometimes uncontrollable functions (as all Golding's work has done). These elements of style and theme disturbed, as perhaps they were intended to, and their use seemed not merely over-insistent but even deliberately exhibitionist. The time sequence, too, created problems – it was difficult to grasp the significance of the order of events at first reading, and there were a number of moving and memorable passages, such as the Mountjoys' lodger dying of lung cancer, which were not sufficiently connected with the book's overall plan.

In *Free Fall* Golding, it seemed, had displayed that most un-English of characteristics, over-writing. That he acknowledged as much may be gathered from his lecture to the students of UCLA cited earlier, where he remarked 'Faults of excess seem to me more forgivable than faults of coldness, at least in the exercise of craftsmanship.'[5] His American audiences were more likely to accept this assertion than his own countrymen. George Steiner once argued[6] that archetypal books such as *Moby Dick* and *Pride and Prejudice* are as much the product of geography as history – the one big in conception, theme and style as befits a big country and a pioneer society; the other excelling in a close analysis of the social scene, in keeping with a small, closely-knit island community. According to this account, the European novel surrounds itself with the real, documenting the actual world: its main current is prosaic, its field deliberately narrowed. It is secular in outlook, rejecting the mystical and supernatural and placing a high value on rationality. Classic American literature, by contrast, is more metaphysical. Some of the greatest American novelists – Melville and Hawthorne for example – are concerned with the realm of the unconscious and make much more evident use of allegory and symbol. The paradox of Golding's situation began to become apparent after the publication of *Free Fall:* though he was an Englishman to his boots, obviously devoted to the English countryside, and with a literary ancestry that, while varied, was firmly rooted in the British tradition, he had nevertheless been most successful when writing, in Steiner's terms, like an American. When his canvas was large and he was dealing with the remote, the bizarre, the apocalyptic, he seemed entirely in control. Now with *Free Fall* he had dealt directly and for the first time with normal human relationships in a contemporary setting, and though the larger themes were still present, the narrower context had encouraged his readers and critics to expect a conventionality they did not find.

From this perspective, Golding's next novel was to be the test case and, in a sense, his whole status as a major writer seemed to rest on the verdict. Would the doubts raised by *Free Fall* be reinforced? Did the five year gap that had followed it (and there were rumours of re-writing and abandoned works) mean a loss of direction, even, perhaps, a loss of that freshness of vision which had been so characteristic of his early works? Or did it mean, as all who had admired Golding hoped, that the new ground however uncertainly broken in *Free Fall* would, when thoroughly worked over, provide the basis for a new and more coherent vision?

It was against this background of speculation that *The Spire* finally appeared. The reaction to it came as something of an anti-climax. The book was fairly well received by the popular reviewers, apparently sold well and, in the Honours lists that so many newpapers like to publish around Christmas time, was duly voted one of the books of the year. Yet on the whole critical reaction was guarded, even cool, and in the British critical journals in particular Golding lost his case by default. A typical reaction was that of *The Critical Quarterly* which announced as soon as the book was published that an article on it would appear in the following issue, then apologised and reannounced it for a future issue, and finally quietly dropped the project altogether.

As with *Free Fall*, uncertainty as to the book's merits focused

on two issues – the obliqueness of the narration which seemed
perversely obscure and indirect, and the style which was as
eccentric and highly mannered as ever. Only two pages into the
novel the following passage occurred:

> The chancellor had found what he was looking for, a
> memory.
> 'Ah yes.'
> Then, in ancient busyness, he crept away over the pave-
> ment to the door and through it. He left a message, in the
> air behind him.
> 'Mattins. Of course.'
> Jocelin stood still, and shot an arrow of love after him.

For many, it was too much. As far as British critics were
concerned, the wilderness years lay ahead for Golding. In
1966, in *The Bluffer's Guide to Literature,* Martin Seymour-
Smith could write 'Treat *Lord of the Flies* as seminal, but refuse
to talk about his later novels – thus anticipating fashion which
is turning faintly against him.' Such a gem of instant erudition
in a light-hearted pamphlet need not be taken too seriously,
yet, like all safe judgements, it contains a grain of truth. For a
long time thereafter Golding was out of fashion. His next
novel, *The Pyramid,* in 1967, attracted little attention and less
admiration; nor did the three short stories published as *The
Scorpion God* in 1971. Then for a long time there was silence,
broken only by the news of Golding's Pincher-Martin style
near-disaster in a boating accident in the Channel.

It took another bestseller and Booker prize winner, *Rites of
Passage* – a book full of resonances yet essentially simple in
form and with a comparatively straightforward narrative line
– to restore general interest in Golding. Its success obviously
delighted him. And it certainly delighted those of his critics,
more often American than British, who had been unwavering
in their belief that he was one of the very best talents still
writing. It was good to see Golding back in the public eye

again, giving interviews to the press, appearing on television, speaking at length in his simple, direct, slightly self-deprecating way about most of his published work – with one significant exception: a year before *Rites of Passage* appeared, Golding had published another novel, *Darkness Visible*, a book so different from the Booker prize winner that it was hard to believe that they had both come from the same pen at almost the same time. Whereas *Rites of Passage* was all spontaneity and ease, the only confident assertion one could make about *Darkness Visible* was that it was the product of immense labour and must surely have occupied Golding for many of the intervening 12 years since the appearance of *The Pyramid*. And Golding would not talk about it. 'The fact of the matter is,' he commented privately, 'that for a number of reasons *Darkness Visible* is the one of my books I have refused to talk about: and the more I have been pressed, the more stubborn my refusal has become.'[7] It is not difficult to imagine what some of those reasons were. Golding had chosen for its title a notorious oxymoron, and it is certainly clear that many general readers found the book deeply and relentlessly obscure. Grappling with a complexity whose depths could not perhaps finally be plumbed, it is scarcely surprising that Golding has been reluctant to produce a checklist of clues such as T.S. Eliot obligingly (if misleadingly) produced for *The Waste Land*.

It would be a pity, however, if such an omission were to distract attention from *Darkness Visible* and the recognition of its central importance to an understanding of Golding's work. For though it was *Rites of Passage* that proved that Golding could still write a bestselling novel, it was *Darkness Visible* that provided the main evidence as to how and why Golding's approach to writing had changed after (perhaps even during) the creation of *Pincher Martin*. To what extent this was a conscious process is something that can only be guessed at. We know from the lecture he gave at UCLA that Golding *did* change his mind about the status of authorial interpretation. Such a shift of attitude is unlikely to have been the outcome of

an intellectual conversion to the Lawrentian dictum 'Never
trust the artist: trust the tale.' More probably, it formed a part
of his natural development as a writer. A man as intensely
committed to the numinous as Golding could hardly have
continued to use the tight polemical framework of *Lord of the
Flies* and *The Inheritors* indefinitely. The words of Ecclesiastes,
that 'for the mind of man, God has appointed mystery, that
man may never fathom God's own purpose from beginning to
end' would find a ready echo in Golding's mind, though he
would probably add that the urge to make darkness visible, to
express the inexpressible, to create myths where certainties
fail, remains our chief preoccupation. From a very early age
Golding had shown himself to be more than usually intolerant
of total explanations, whether they came from the scientist,
the anthropologist, the sociologist or any other specialist.

   Golding has described himself standing as a child before a
painted Egyptian sarcophagus, trying to meet the focus of its
eyes because they inhabited a face 'prepared to penetrate
mysteries, . . . prepared to go down and through, in darkness';
yet he also knew that such intimate communion with a thing
that 'dwells with a darkness that is its light' if it were possible
would only be possible in death; at the same time he recognised in the very presence of the Egyptian relic 'my own
mournful staring into the darkness, my own savage grasp on
life'.[8] In his essay 'The Ladder and the Tree' we find him, like
Oliver in *The Pyramid*, acquiescing to his parents' passionate
desire that he should go to Oxford to read science, while
resigned to the fact that science could tell him nothing that he
really wanted to know:[9]

> My career was to be a scientific one. Science was busy
> clearing up the universe. There was no place in this
> exquisitely logical universe for the terrors of darkness.
> There was darkness, of course, but it was just darkness,
> the absence of light; had none of the looming terror,
> which I knew night-long in my very bones . . .

Rules, declensions, paradigms and vocabularies stretched before me. They were like a ladder which I knew now I should climb, rung after factual rung, and Sir James Jeans and Professor Einstein were waiting at the top to sign me on. I was glad about science in a remote sort of way. If you were going to be anything, then a scientist was what you ought to be. But the ladder was so long. In this dreary mood of personal knowledge and prophecy I knew that I should climb it; knew too that the darkness was all around, inexplicable, unexorcised, haunted, a gulf across which the ladder lay without reaching to the light.

Both these autobiographical accounts reveal Golding's fascination with the idea of darkness and the various interpretations it could have. At one extreme is the version he abhors most – the scientist's mere 'absence of light', that current ignorance or state of imperfect knowledge which, we are promised, will be banished by the new dawn, when the task of clearing up the universe is completed. Darkness can also be associated with a 'looming terror' which haunts the dreams, motivates the actions of men, and proves that Satan is still loose in the world. And at the other extreme, darkness becomes something different altogether – the mystery into which and through which one must go if one is to find God, whoever or whatever God may be.

From the perspective of three decades it is now possible to see that darkness has been Golding's theme all along and that a book dealing with the final arbitration between darkness and light would one day be inevitable. For if the intensity and subtlety with which Golding has probed that mystery has changed over the years, the preoccupation with its ambiguities and complexities has been there from the very first book. When Ralph, at the end of *Lord of the Flies* weeps 'for the end of innocence, the darkness of man's heart', the reader assumes that 'darkness' here refers to the dark or evil side of man's nature. And in a sense it does. Golding has always shown himself to be more than usually aware of the central paradox of human existence whereby man's capacity to aspire (what Golding has called his sense of 'My Godness') is constantly threatened by the 'broken-down criminality' of his nature, the curse he brought from Eden. But the juxtaposing and opposing of the words 'innocence' and 'darkness' suggests that the word 'darkness' also connotes 'experience' and this, in its turn, can be understood in two ways. In its narrow sense, experience stands for the adult point of view as against the uncorrupted vision of the child. It is one of the ironies of *Lord of the Flies* that the 'true, wise friend called Piggy' who has consistently protested about the boys 'acting like kids' should himself be destroyed because the boys have taken his advice and organised themselves to fight like grown-ups. In its wider sense (and both narrow and wide are implicit) 'experience' is used to refer to the universal experience of mankind, that is, of the loss of innocence, exchanged for the dubious benefits of civilisation, itself embodied in the myth of the fall.

The theme of darkness in *Lord of the Flies* is given additional weight by appearing right at the end of the book, it being Golding's practice in the early works to use the climax as a means of dramatising the ironies which were part of his didactic purpose. The point is more clearly made in *The Inheritors*. To the new men, through whose eyes at the end of the book we see the final destruction of the Neanderthals, the darkness inhabited by the strange creatures ('they live in darkness under the trees') is that of ignorance, of the unknown and of terror – the natural habitat of the bogey men who will haunt their descendants' dreams. But for Golding, who invites us to see Neanderthal man from the inside, the real darkness is the bleak and uncertain future into which the new men sail away:

Tuami looked at the line of darkness. It was far away there was plenty of water in between. He peered forward past the sail to see what lay at the other end of the lake, but it was so long, and there was such a flashing from the water that he could not see if the line of darkness had an ending.

Yet by and large in their treatment of darkness Golding's first two books do not offer close correspondences to that awesome boyhood experience, when he had looked into the Egyptian mummy's eye and felt the scalp-tingling sensation of a gaze which was 'prepared to go down and through, in darkness', into a central mystery whose exploration was at once dangerous and yet held the promise of a new mode of understanding. As a writer, Golding undertook its first tentative exploration in *Pincher Martin* and, in the process, began to change into a different type of novelist. *Pincher Martin*, after *The Pyramid* the most underrated of Golding's novels, was greeted when it appeared on the one hand with incomprehension and on the other with criticisms of being too clever by half. Golding professed himself surprised at the general response and particularly by the difficulties some readers found in understanding it. He had planned the novel in great detail and with considerable care. He had put in all the necessary information. He had made his central character as bad as he possibly could be, so that there would be no doubt as to what was happening. As he put it:[10]

> I fell over backwards making that novel explicit. I said to myself, 'Now here is going to be a novel, it's going to be a blow on behalf of the ordinary universe, which I think on the whole likely to be the right one, and I'm going to write it so vividly and accurately and with such an exact programme that nobody can possibly mistake exactly what I mean.'

Despite his efforts, its drift had not been obvious and he had been astonished as well as wryly amused at the number of people who had identified with Pincher and had said, in effect,

'That's me.' Golding himself found some explanation of this in the Promethean element that had crept into the portrayal of his central character, and suspected that admiration for his elemental battle to survive had aroused this unintended response.

But a far more fundamental process was at work in the book. The poet in Golding was taking over from the story-teller, the poetic symbol from the prosaic idea, and all sorts of effects were being generated over which he had less than full control and whose complexity was steadily increasing. The clearest indication of this was provided by the ending which, following Golding's previous practice, was designed to change the reader's viewpoint (everyone thought the book had been about a sailor's desperate struggle for survival, and lo and behold he had been dead since page two). But far from illuminating the book's meaning, the ending seemed a cheap *coup de théâtre* since its only purpose was to alert the imperceptive reader to the true nature of Pincher Martin's plight. More to the point, the *real* ending (as the later Golding would instinctively have known) had occurred several pages earlier with the final image of Pincher reduced to a pair of ragged claws yet still fighting his last battle with that darkness which symbolised no outward condition, but rather the dark night of the soul itself, the sombre limbo between this life and the surrender to something beyond. This was the poetic resolution of the book, and its complexity and subtlety were too great for the tightly controlled and ordered structure which Golding had imposed on it. The straitjacket of form was never to dominate his work in that way again.

It was in *Free Fall* that Golding first set about the immense task of investigating the nature of darkness itself. The opening pages are peppered with references, both direct and oblique, to the darkness that lies behind experience, and which it is the writer's duty, however fumblingly and inadequately, to explore. Like all explorations, it induces a sense of deprivation and isolation. Only four pages into the book, Sammy, its narrator declares:

Our loneliness is the loneliness not of the cell or the castaway; it is the loneliness of that dark thing that sees as at the atom furnace by reflection, feels by remote control and hears only words phoned to it in a foreign tongue.

And in case there is any remaining doubt as to the difficulty of the task on which he is embarking, Sammy immediately continues:

My darkness reaches out and fumbles at a typewriter with its tongs. Your darkness reaches out with your tongs and grasps a book.

As if conscious that such an enigmatic utterance should not appear so early in the story, Sammy adds the question, 'Do I exasperate by translating incoherence into incoherence?' He has a point, for although we have been given an early oblique reference to the 'terror of the blacked-out cell' which is to focus Sammy's real insight into darkness, we tend to feel, if not exasperation, at least a certain puzzlement as to what all the fuss is about. At first the darkness he refers to seems to be just the old familiar second term of the innocence/experience dichotomy previously explored in *Lord of the Flies* and *The Inheritors*. Sammy claims to be 'looking for the beginning of responsibility, the beginning of darkness, the point where I began'; and many of the earlier episodes in the novel seem designed to reveal the lightness and innocence surrounding 'the little boy, clear as spring water', as compared with the darkness and experience of 'the man like a stagnant pool'. Outwardly, Sammy's struggle in the book is towards understanding and some kind of synthesis between the worlds of fact and spirit, but he reluctantly concludes at the end that this is impossible – that 'there is no bridge' and that (in the words of the old song referred to in a later novel) 'one is one and all alone and ever more shall be so.'

But this is only Sammy's view. Actually the investigation of the nature of darkness is much more complex. Something happens in the novel, possibly even without the author being fully conscious of it, not altogether different from what happened to Blake in the course of composing the *Songs of Innocence* and *Songs of Experience*. Blake's purpose in writing the sequence was obscure and may not lightly be defined in a sentence or two; but the poems reveal his recognition that not only is it impossible to understand the two contrary states in isolation, it is also impossible to evaluate them independently of one another. Thus innocence itself seems flawed and unsatisfactory at times, simply because it has not been subjected to the refining fire of experience. And the apparent simplicity of Sammy's quest in *Free Fall* contains within it a similar anomaly: crucial to this theme is what happens when, as a prisoner-of-war, he is placed by his Gestapo interrogator in a completely blacked-out cell. There the darkness breeds in him unimaginable terrors and the soft object discovered by his probing hands and feet at the centre of the cell becomes the focus for his most fearful thoughts. But the final outcome of this experience is quite the reverse of what his worldly and cultivated interrogator had intended. When he is released, Sammy is as 'a man resurrected', seeing the common everyday things of the prison camp around him magically transmuted by the experience, so that for the first time in his adult life he knows peace and can say:

> Everything is related to everything else and all relationship is either discord or harmony. The power of gravity, dimension and space, the movement of the earth and sun and unseen stars, these made what might be called music and I heard it.

Golding returns to this moment and to what happened on Sammy's release from the darkness and horror of the prison cell on the last page of the novel. When the cell door is opened and the light floods in, the source of his terror is revealed as nothing more than a damp floorcloth some guard had forgotten to remove. It is with this symbol, figuring the difference between appearance and reality, that we are left. Sammy might ponder over the Commandant's words, 'The Herr Doctor does not know about peoples', but poetically the meaning is clear. Through his ordeal by darkness, darkness had been made visible and become a source of revelation. He had, if only for a brief moment, perceived that everything was related to everything else, that the movement of earth, sun and unseen stars made what might be called music. And he had heard it.

Free Fall, then, displays a new type of writing in which the direction the book takes is governed less by its actual programme (that is, Sammy's view of things) than by its own inner necessities; a type of writing in which themes begin to dominate ideas, and poetry prose. Of course in one sense Golding has always written a highly-coloured kind of prose which had many affinities with poetry in its verbal precision, its mellifluousness and richness of imagery. His first published work was not a novel but the traditional slim volume of poems written 'in an inferior manner' to 'the more accessible romantics', for which he received five pounds and no encouragement to write more. Golding now endorses the publisher's implied view that he was not meant to be a poet, but the urge to poetry has remained and found an outlet in other ways. Like Browning who needed to compose a sequence of plays in order to discover that his true *métier* was the dramatic monologue, Golding's poetic impulse is most fully realised not in the scattered patches of fine writing in the early works (of which the passage describing Simon's body being carried out to sea in *Lord of the Flies* is probably the most powerful) but in the later works where a whole book may rely for its effectiveness on the reader's ability to pick up and relate a tangle of allusions in a way more readily associated with the verbal complexity of poetic form.

When in 1967 I published the article on which the next
chapter's account of *The Spire* is largely based, its conclusion
ran as follows:

> What is remarkable about Golding's handling of the
> theme compared with that in *The Inheritors* is not only the
> greater element of ingenuity (though that is undoubtedly
> there) but the fact that what 'argument' there is, is so
> unobtrusive, so intricately controlled, so layered in
> depth, that it reveals itself fully and satisfyingly only, as a
> poem does, in terms of the images and symbols out of
> which it is constructed.
>
> And this finally is what makes *The Spire* Golding's most
> impressive work so far. It is not a book without faults and
> it is easy, in the thrill of the chase for a solution, to forget
> how irritating some of Golding's attitudes and verbal
> mannerisms continue to be. But it also marks a
> significant advance in his work in that it is the first of his
> books to escape completely from the thraldom of the
> prosaic 'idea' which has always, to a greater or lesser
> extent, tended to keep his novels straining hard but never
> quite getting off the ground. *The Spire* succeeds at a level
> that one feels Golding has always aspired to but never
> before reached – that of the dramatic poem, and it may
> well be a decisive indication that, in terms of his work as
> a novelist, the best is yet to be.

Looking back, this judgement now seems inadequate (how
could *Lord of the Flies* and *The Inheritors* be described as 'never
quite getting off the ground?'), but such an apologia needs to
be judged against the background of growing indifference to
Golding's writing in the late 1960s; it was inspired by the
conviction that *The Spire* had not received its due. Compared
with anything Golding had written before, it was hugely
complex, and the density (even, at times, obscurity) of the
prose reflected the struggle to communicate which, in Sammy

Mountjoy's words, 'is our passion and our despair.' Besides inventing myths himself, Golding was now underpinning his themes by obliquely incorporating mythological patterns from other cultures and this, together with a general rich allusiveness, demanded from the reader a width of reading and sustained attention if the book was to be fully understood. Nevertheless the story line remained simple enough to be appreciated as much for what it was as for its deep underlay of allusion – something that could not equally be claimed for *Free Fall*. In this sense, *The Spire* seemed to provide evidence of a major development in Golding's work.

Yet when *The Pyramid* appeared in 1967 this major change of direction seemed merely to have run into the sand. Among Golding enthusiasts there had been a feeling of excitement and anticipation when the title of his next novel became known. An essay in *The Hot Gates* two years before revealed that ancient Egypt had always been one of Golding's greatest loves – indeed, at the age of seven, he had set himself the task of writing a play about it.[11] It seemed likely not only that the new novel would be set there, but also that the author might incorporate Egyptian mythology as successfully as he had done Teutonic myth in *The Spire*. Instead what did one get? A light-hearted social comedy about English provincial life, though concluding on a more sombre note, apparently intended to entertain and, in so far as it had any further purpose, to take a hard look at British class structure. That there was more to it is argued in a later chapter. But its sheer surprise value provided a salutary lesson on the dangers of trying to force a creative writer into a pre-ordained scheme of one's own choosing. Golding has always actively resisted any such stereotyping: 'I have always felt that a writer's books should be as different from each other as possible,'[12] he has recently declared. And also, 'My approach to a novel, then, is a confusion in itself, a hand-to-mouth thing. Men do not write the books they should, they write the books they can.'[13] Of no book is this more obviously true than *The Pyramid*. It includes indications (and others were to appear in the short story 'The Scorpion God') that he might one day produce a great novel about ancient Egypt. He is conscious of its relevance to our predicament and believes that, living as we do in an age of 'fragment and wreckage', the remnants of that ancient civilisation might yet[14]

> convey by a meta-language what we have left for a future and what we may build on . . . It may be that in a reading of these broken stones lies an image of a creature maimed yet engaged to time and our world and enduring it with a purpose no man knows and an effect that no man can guess.

But there is another possibility – that Golding has already attempted this giant task in *Darkness Visible*. If so, he has not, as he may once have intended, used the fragments of ancient Egypt and its beliefs, but the living myths of Judaism and Christianity which have more directly conditioned our culture and our whole way of being. For if *Free Fall* was an investigation of the nature of that darkness which is the sign of life's mystery, and if *The Spire* provided some resolution which, by assimilating terror and joy, offered hope to us as individual human beings, *Darkness Visible* has attempted to deal with the same theme in cosmic terms. Its protagonist, Matty, is not only the first of Golding's so-called 'saint' figures to play a central role, but is quite literally 'a creature maimed yet engaged to time and our world and enduring it with a purpose no man knows and an effect that no man can guess'. The central role given to this strange, other-worldly figure and to the final conflict between the forces of darkness and the forces of light in which he is engaged, is at once the mark of the novel's difference from the rest and of its major importance in the canon of Golding's work. Appropriately, in the light of its title, it could be seen as Golding's own *Paradise Lost*, the novel that above all others pleased him, 'long choosing and beginning late', and which, in terms of sheer scope and endeavour must surely rank with any produced this century.

Golding's capacity to surprise was demonstrated yet again when, having produced such a large and obviously exhausting masterpiece, within the space of a year and with little apparent effort he published another novel so different as to suggest that it had afforded a rest from the labours of *Darkness Visible*. For all its obvious merits, *Rites of Passage* has an air of relaxation, and in it Golding returns to the novelist's primary task of telling a good story well, graphically and very dramatically. He also reverts to some of the devices used in the earlier novels: the simple question that provides a starting point (what circumstance could cause a man to die of shame?), and the change of viewpoint when the same events are seen through different eyes. Golding evidently did not find it difficult to write; after the depths of *Darkness Visible* it seems to have flown easily from his pen, as he explained to James Baker in a recent interview:[15]

> It . . . was great fun for me. I happened to have a great deal of source material in my head. I didn't have to bother to do any research or anything like that, and, you see, I know sailors, I know the Royal Navy.

At another point in the same interview he even suggested that both here and in *The Scorpion God* he was 'to some extent . . . sending up the idea of history' and had his tongue in his cheek 'much more often than people ever suspect because I have this kind of solemn reputation'.[16]

In order to see the book's action in comic terms, however, one would have to ignore most of its other implications and tonalities, including that conveyed so awesomely in Talbot's last words to his illustrious patron:

> With lack of sleep and too much understanding I grow a little crazy, I think, like all men at sea who live too close

to each other and too close thereby to all that is monstrous under the sun and moon.

The sombre tone of such a remark (itself untypical of the person who makes it) and its key placing right at the end of the book suggest that, whatever Golding's intentions, something else had intervened, something that pervades the later novels as a whole. It is not just that a quarter of a century's extra living has given Golding a more penetrating insight into the darkness of man's heart than perhaps he recognises, but rather that such insights continue to manifest themselves most characteristically in the rich language of poetic suggestion rather than in the confident assertions of the narrative. Underneath the black comedy of early nineteenth-century seafaring life, the dark places of the heart, the cellar, the cell and the pit, yawn just as hungrily as they had done in *Darkness Visible*.

In Golding's view the artist must aim for a 'passionate insight'; he must 'dive down through the complexities of living to find a curious creature not usually found on the surface';[17] he must attempt to illuminate the further side of darkness. This task has been performed under the sternest of threats, for throughout his career as a novelist man has possessed the means to wipe himself and all his tribe off the face of the earth, and Golding has never forgotten this. Before the action of *Lord of the Flies* began, an atomic war had taken place; Golding's horrified descriptions of it were cut away from the final version. And in the opening pages of *Darkness Visible*, Matty walks out of a firestorm that might be the end of the world and is certainly redolent of Milton's hell, a place of 'hideous ruin and combustion'. His novels are heartfelt pleas that we should root out the panic and hatred, the seeds of war within us; and his frail witnesses are words, uncertain of their own load-bearing capacity, as Sammy's anxious introduction to *Free Fall* reveals: 'We are dumb and blind yet we must see and speak.'

The need to see, to speak and to set down become heavier compulsions in Golding's later work, and from Sammy Mountjoy onwards, the act of recording becomes a significant element in the search for understanding. *Rites of Passage* unfolds in the form of one journal inside another. Edmund Talbot and poor Colley, like the barely educated Matty of *Darkness Visible* ('I have bought this book to write in and a biro because of what happened . . .') confide their lives and themselves to their journals. Golding too, it seems, now keeps a journal and is intrigued by and uneasily conscious of how far diarists 'give away their game'; 'it is not merely the closeness of the pen to the subject, it is the minuteness of the strokes,' he comments.[18] This minuteness is at once a guarantee of authenticity but also a limitation. The journal is a record of a single, partial, isolated view, so that Matty's Blake-like visions must be balanced against Sophy's nihilism, Colley's sense of the numinous by Talbot's reductive logic. Records of experience, however true to the feeling of the moment of setting down, can only be one pebble in the artist's larger mosaic. Dean Jocelin had written an account of his original vision of the spire as a prayer made visible, and had locked it away where his heart was, 'in the old chest . . . in the left hand corner'. But when Father Adam reads it back to him, it seems to have become irrelevant: 'What does this explain? Nothing! Nothing!' As if consciously recapitulating Jocelin's action, Golding too set out his conception of *The Spire* in a prelude, part of which he has reprinted in his essay 'A Moving Target',[19] though he subsequently abandoned it. It had come to seem to him no more relevant to the book he had finally written than Jocelin's testament seemed to the completed spire.

The very act of writing involves a commitment that is potentially dangerous, for the writer does more than make a recorded promise ('there was nothing in writing,' Pincher insists); he weaves himself into his web of words, he builds himself 'in with the rest of them', and so makes it easier for an uncreative academe to pin him down beneath his own achievement by dwelling on its repetitions rather than its renewals. And the nuisance value of inqusitive academics who would pluck out the heart of his mystery is the lighter end of a more serious disquiet about the complicity of the artist with the darkness he records, a complicity that first found full expression in *The Spire;* later the character called 'the Liar' in *The Scorpion God* pointed in the direction of Plato's rejection of the artist's fictions. Doubts of this kind find their fullest expression in Golding's most recent novel, *The Paper Men.* Here the effect of the written word is to surround the anti-hero Barclay with a sticky cocoon of his recorded sins and failures that simultaneously trap him and expose him. The ultimate commitment of putting things 'in writing' acquires overtones of a Faustian pact as Barclay is tempted to sign away his own life by consenting to the writing of an official, an authorised biography. Like Jocelin, the artist of *The Paper Men* is not merely judging but judged; his work is submitted not merely to the censure of the London literary scene but to a higher, calmer gaze. Like Jocelin, Barclay comes to find out where he is and what he has done, but unlike Jocelin, he cannot plead a higher cause, an achievement worthy of the human cost. Barclay's torments, like Pincher's, spring from a consuming self-interest and his terror of heights is opposed to Jocelin's fearless clambering up his own spire. Barclay's fear reflects his far greater guilt, as the unfocused phantasmagoric quality of the writing reflects Barclay's barren self-absorption. Locked in the prison of his ego, nothing and no one possess reality for him, and for the artist nothing can come of nothing. There is no way out of this hollow man's twilit world, death's dream kingdom.

Golding knows, perhaps too well, what it is to be a writer teased by gadfly critics and his knowledge has left too little space for the operation of that animating imagination which is his peculiar and privileged strength. Wilf Barclay, bound into his own book, imprisoned within the accumulating papers that he cannot bring himself to throw away, is at once too near and too far from Bill Golding; he is a Golding emptied of his creator's most vital and essential quality – his absorbed gaze at the world around him, his fatal and heroic curiosity as to the true nature of his fellow-men:[20]

What man is, whatever man is under the eye of heaven, that I burn to know and that – I do not say this lightly – I would endure knowing. The themes closest to my purpose, to my imagination have stemmed from that preoccupation, have been of such a sort that they might move me a little nearer that knowledge.

1

The Spire
(1964)

> We have a primitive belief that virtue, force, power –
> what the anthropologist might call *mana* – lie in the
> original stones and nowhere else. Yet we must know
> these stones; they must be part of daily life so that we
> may have adjusted some sensor to the correct wavelength
> for reception, as you might adjust your eyes to a dim
> light.

Golding's essay 'An Affection for Cathedrals',[1] published a
year after *The Spire*, provides an indirect explanation of how he
came to write the novel. He records his intense response to the
stones of Salisbury cathedral, his gut-reaction to the very
fabric of the building. Once he had tuned himself in to the
right frequency and he could hear the stones singing, the
story of *The Spire* must have unfolded before his inner ear, or
eye. It is clear, whatever embellishments Golding may have
added, that the main story is based on the actual construction
of the spire at Salisbury in the early fourteenth century. Even
the names of the two protagonists, Jocelin and Roger, are
taken from two former bishops of the earlier foundation, Old
Sarum, whose bodies are entombed under the same arch in
the present cathedral. By itself, of course, this would have
little significance, since one would expect an author writing
about the construction of a spire to avail himself of any local

information there was, and what more natural than that Golding should look to the cathedral he had known and loved from childhood.

There are four good additional reasons, however, why it had to be Salisbury rather than any other cathedral. In the first place, Salisbury has the highest spire of all the English cathedrals (404 feet as against the 400 feet of Golding's spire) and its height is an essential element of the theme of the book. Secondly, and this is equally necessary for the book's purpose, the spire was only added a hundred years after the building of the cathedral itself and does not seem to have been part of the original plan. Because of this, the constructional problems must have been immense, and the building of the Salisbury spire is generally reckoned as an early engineering marvel, employing many ingenious techniques for spreading the enormous weight of the steeple, such as masonry flyers and hidden bands of wrought iron reinforcement. As early as 1417, in the reign of Henry V, the spire was found to be in a dangerous state; by 1689 it was estimated to be 22 inches out of the perpendicular, due to settlement in the piers on the western side of the tower; yet the spire still stood and continues to stand. And this leads to the third reason why it had to be Salisbury – namely that the whole construction of tower and spire was something of a miracle, not only because the original building was unsuited to receive them, but also because the cathedral itself was founded on nothing more substantial than a spongy bog. As late as 1899, the Victorian architect Francis Bond could still talk of the 'wanton carelessness' of the original builders and the 'foolhardy enterprise' of adding the spire, thus proving that the doubting spirit of Roger Mason, the master builder, lived on and that Golding had chosen well in using this particular construction as the basis of his myth.

Finally, it had to be Salisbury cathedral not just because of the uniqueness of its constructional features but because of its proximity to what Golding has called the 'cathedral' of that prehistoric metropolis where the roads along the old chalk

Downs meet – Stonehenge.² The confrontation between these two ancient edifices, one Christian and one pagan, is essential to Golding's purpose, providing him with an additional dimension and accounting for a good deal of the book's richness of texture.

Like other Golding novels, *The Spire* relies for its full effect on its power to evoke echoes of a variety of works, with varying degrees of significance. In some cases such echoes arouse little more than the sense of recognition: the Anselm of the book, for instance, may be distantly related to the Anselm ('Is Anselm keeping back?') of Browning's poem, 'The Bishop orders his tomb at Saint Praxed's'; the theme of Browning's poem obviously has some relevance to the relationship between Jocelin and his aunt, the Lady Alison. But this remains only an echo – an embellishment which adds little of significance to what is already there. On the other hand, the myth of Balder provides an important underpinning to the construction of *The Spire*, as the Grail legend had done for *The Waste Land*, and any full reading should take some account of it.

Another work which may be relevant as a source is Ibsen's *The Master Builder*, the powerful and moving play which was inspired by the chance of love that came to Ibsen late in life when he was holidaying at Gossensass. The issue should have been clear-cut. Ibsen at the time was a man in his prime, happily married, famous, successful and widely respected. But the incident revealed tensions in himself that he did not know existed, and the ambiguity of his response is objectified in the play chiefly through the symbol of the spire. Solness, the master builder, had in his youth been a builder of churches, but now he has settled for respectability and affluence, designing housing estates. Into this situation comes a young woman, Hilde, who as a schoolgirl had witnessed his ascent of the spire of her local church, had fallen in love with him, and now offers him that love and the challenge to build again. Solness accepts the challenge and the play ends with his falling to his death after attempting to scale the spire of his own house.

This ending, at once futile and tragic, and at the same time full of power, serenity and a sense of achievement, depends for its effect on the symbol of the spire which not only indicates in the most brutally obvious way the youthful virility which Solness was a fool to think he could recapture, but also the compulsion to accept the larger dare to body, mind and spirit which alone gives meaning to life. To say this, however, is merely to expose the inadequacy of any attempt to attach precise significance to an experience which for Solness, as for Ibsen, could only partly be understood. A comparable sense of the inadequacy of words to explain the complexity of motives moved Golding to take the exploration a stage further, so that some of the preoccupations of the play seem to be caught up in the novel; it is one of the marks of its greatness that one is not immediately aware that a change of level has taken place.

Superficially *The Spire* is about a conflict between Faith and Reason, and at its profoundest levels it is still concerned with that conflict. In between it is about many other things. In this case, faith is represented by Jocelin, the dean, and the sense of his isolation as a result is established from the first page of the book. Jocelin has had a vision which prompts him to build a spire to the greater glory of God; everybody else is against it. The other clerics are opposed to the idea to a man, some because of jealousy and distrust of the dean, some because of the losses both spiritual and pecuniary which will result from the interruption of the regular services of the church, and others simply because any form of change is to be resisted. Pangall the old caretaker – lame, misshapen, a left-over from the past – is against it because he resents the mess, the upset in his quiet household, and the intrusion of the foul-mouthed workmen who make him a butt for their jokes. Finally and more significantly, the master builder himself, Roger Mason, is against it because his craft tells him that the spire that Jocelin envisages just cannot be built. Provision for a spire was not part of the original plan of the cathedral and he estimates that the foundations are inadequate to support such

a massive structure. From the beginning, Jocelin recognises
that Roger is the only opponent who really matters. The rest
can be humoured: Roger must be opposed. He must be persuaded that the truths of reason are unimportant in comparison to the truths of the spirit:

> 'The building is a diagram of prayer; and our spire will be
> a diagram of the highest prayer of all . . . the folly isn't
> mine. It's God's Folly. Even in the old days he never asked
> men to do what was reasonable.'

Partly because of Jocelin's importunity, partly because his
army of workmen need employment and no other work is
available (Jocelin has already seen to this), and partly because
of the attractions of Pangall's young, red-haired wife Goody,
Roger agrees to put the work in hand. A pit is dug at the
crossways of the cathedral to examine the foundations, a wall
is broken down at the end of one of the transepts to allow
easier access, and the roof is opened up in preparation for the
building of the tower. Then occurs an incident which precipi-
tates one of those moments of high drama that Golding han-
dles so well. The search for foundations reveals that there are
none; the cathedral is floating on a sea of mud. As the digging
strikes into it, huge pressures build up which threaten the
fabric of the building and the pit has to be hastily filled with
anything that comes to hand. To Roger, the incident is decisive; there must be no spire because only a madman would
attempt such a construction in such circumstances. To Jocelin, however, it is merely something which can be summarised
in a formula he is to use repeatedly as the building proceeds –
'the lesson for this level'. He still has no doubts that the spire
can be built, but now realises that there may be a necessary
price to be paid, by Roger as well as himself:

> You and I were chosen to do this thing together. It's a
> great glory. I see now it'll destroy us of course. What are

we, after all? Only I tell you this, Roger, with the whole strength of my soul. The thing can be built and will be built, in the very teeth of Satan . . . only you and I, my son, my friend, when we've done tormenting ourselves and each other, will know what stones and beams and lead and mortar went into it.

Nothing can be allowed to stand in the way of the building. Jocelin knows that Roger is becoming desperately involved with Goody Pangall and there are good reasons why, as a man and as a priest, he should yield to Roger's plea to remove him from the area of temptation; but he also knows that the entanglement is the strongest force keeping Roger at his task and is prepared to regard even this as a means to the greater good:

'I am about my Father's business.'

Pangall, the old caretaker, is being driven to distraction, for the superstitious workmen believe the spire to be ill-omened and are using him as a scapegoat to ward off impending disaster. When the earth creeps and Jocelin still refuses to abandon the building, a riot breaks out in the cathedral in which Pangall is apparently hunted from the place, never to return. Jocelin, preoccupied with his spire, finds the episode merely alarming and is wilfully blind to the enormity of what has, in reality, happened to Pangall.

What services remain have been transferred to the Lady Chapel at the end of the cathedral, but as the dust rises, as the noise increases, as first the tower and then the spire continue to grow, the normal life of the cathedral virtually ceases. For one thing, the people of the town now avoid the building as an unlucky place, fearful of being there when the spire collapses. For another, Jocelin is no longer their priest, since he identifies himself more and more with the ranks of the ungodly who are building the spire. He avoids the company of the other clergy, spends his time exclusively with the workmen high up in the tower, concentrates all his powers on the job of driving the spire up by the force of his will, always sustained (as he believes) by the angel at his back which warms him and assures him of the rightness of his purpose.

But the warmth at his back is not simply an angel – it is also a form of spinal consumption that is slowly destroying him. As time goes on, the spire nears completion and begins to extract it grim toll. Goody Pangall miscarries Roger's child and dies wretchedly. From this moment Roger Mason becomes a drunkard and suicidal melancholic, performing the miracles of engineering that the construction of the spire demands but no longer interested in whether it stands or falls. Jocelin himself drives on as relentlessly as ever but is increasingly consumed with doubts as to whether his motives for causing so much destruction are as uncomplicated as he once thought. It is a very much less confident Jocelin who presents his case to the Visitor from Rome, sent to investigate the complaints about the strange happenings at the cathedral:

'It was so simple at first. On the purely human level, of course, it's a story of shame and folly – Jocelin's Folly, they call it. I had a vision you see, a clear and explicit vision. It was *so* simple! It was to be my work. I was chosen for it. But then the complications began.'

Before discussing what happens when the spire is up and the 'miracle' is tested by the first gales of autumn, it is necessary to consider in greater detail the nature of the 'plant with strange flowers and fruit, complex, twining, engulfing, destroying, strangling' which is Jocelin's image for the 'complications' that have transformed a simple issue into a torment of uncertainty.

Many of these complications are concerned with the purity or otherwise of Jocelin's motives in building the spire, and the validity of his vision. Is the spire, for instance, the cold, pure, geometric abstraction suggested by the formula a 'diagram of prayer', or is it really the phallic weapon, the 'great club', the 'hammer', of his sublimated lust for Goody Pangall? This sexual image is first suggested in the novel by the establishment of a basic analogy:

> The model was like a man lying on his back. The nave was his legs placed together, the transepts on either side were his arms outspread. The choir was his body; and the Lady Chapel where now the services would be held, was his head. And now also, springing, projecting, bursting, erupting from the heart of the building, there was its crown and majesty, the new spire.

Later a process of gradual revelation links Jocelin's relationship with Goody Pangall to the spire itself. When she was a young girl, he had seen her playing games with other girls in the cathedral close, had loved her as his 'daughter in God' with what he thought was 'an unworldly delight', and out of the sense of his own need for her innocence, had arranged the marriage for her with Pangall. What he had concealed from himself was the knowledge that Pangall was impotent and that he was delivering Goody over to him not as a husband but as a eunuch commissioned to protect the object of his master's lust. Goody has known this all along, but for Jocelin the discovery of the true nature of his physical preoccupation with her is as gradual as the slow erection of the spire itself.

At first, the red hair that haunts his dreams can be accepted complacently as the necessary temptation that the priest must undergo in his conflict with the devil; but even at this stage, the association of the experience with the angel that warms as well as the devil that tempts, with the back whose heat is both divine fire and corrupted flesh, anticipates the turbulence that is to come. Soon, as the spire grows and Jocelin's visions torment the more, the illusion he has built up of himself as a sort of Christ in the wilderness ('I do Thy work; and Thou hast sent Thy messenger to comfort me. As it was of old, in the desert') begins to crumble. Desperately and as a last resource he shelters behind the belief that his visions had been prompted by witchcraft, that they were the subtlest form of approach that the devil had yet made. But such superstitious rationalisation will not do, and it remains for Jocelin, on his death-bed, not only to see the experience for what it really is, as something that belongs to him, but to understand, however hazily, that this too may be part of the divine purpose:

> He looked up experimentally to see if at this late hour the witchcraft had left him; and there was a tangle of hair, blazing among the stars; and the great club of his spire lifted towards it. That's all, he thought, that's the explanation if I had time.

As the book proceeds, we are led to question whether the spire is born not out of prayer but out of pride, for again what starts as a fairly modest sin of the spirit at ground level becomes, with the increase of knowledge that the heights bring, a major ambiguity. Thus the element of vanity which is implicit in the carving of the four stone heads of Jocelin to decorate the four sides of the tower seems harmless enough at first. Perhaps the four heads, with their noses like eagles' beaks and the nostrils widely flared like a pair of wings, put a strain on Jocelin's humility, but enough only to raise a rueful smile at this level. It is when the eagle itself is free and ranging in its pride at the tower's rim that the trouble begins. There, everything that belongs to him is seen simultaneously, and pride of possession mingles with a corrupting sense of power – of being above everything, of playing God at a level where gods reside. Jocelin sees the new roads converging on the cathedral and knows it is his spire that has attracted them; he sees his flock reduced to necessary ants below him; he sees their secret sins; he sees the woman watering the milk, the drunkard in the gutter, the bargee who should be delivering his stone taking his ease instead in the local inn; he sees – and, like God, he judges:

> A great anger swamped Jocelin, rage at the drunk man in the gutter and the sot in the Three Tuns. He cried out to Roger's averted face.
> 'My son! You must use my authority. Send a man on a good horse to the Three Tuns. Let him take a whip with him, and let him use it as necessary!'

The dangers of pride and the desire for worldly power are pushed home by the book's setting in the fourteenth century which, as everyone who has read Chaucer or Langland knows, was the great century of church corruption. Golding suggests this in a general way by his reference to the election of the new chancellor, Ivo, who is, in the best tradition of the clergy of the time, a great hunter, and owes his elevation solely to the fact that his father owned the forests from which the beams of the cathedral were made. What is of more importance, however, is that Jocelin himself has apparently secured his own appointment as dean, at a relatively early age and over the heads of the disgruntled Anselms of the time, by a process no less devious and corrupt. In his case, as Jocelin finally discovers to his horror, his Aunt Alison, a favoured mistress of the old king, had urged the king to 'drop a plum in his mouth' out of no better motive than the whim to be generous to a sister she really despised. In view of the fact that it is also Alison's money that is paying for the building of the spire (this time in the hope of buying an honourable resting place for her bones), it brings into question not only Jocelin's standing as a true representative of the cause he serves, but whether bad money can ever be put to good use. For the Church in Rome has responded to Jocelin's appeal for funds with nothing more substantial than the promise of a holy nail; and while on the one hand this carries suggestions of the corrupt practices of characters such as Chaucer's pardoner, with his sack full of pseudo-relics, on the other, it contrasts ironically with the hard cash that comes from Alison's whoring in high places.

And finally it is through the ironic interplay of contrasting elements such as these that Golding gives expression to some of the larger ambiguities surrounding Jocelin's motives for building, and the nature of the building itself. The paradox of the angel at his back who is also the Satan Jocelin has ordered to get behind him, has already been touched on; and that of the nail will be referred to again. But there are others. There is, for instance, the doubt about the supporting pillars of the spire, which give forth a strange music as the pressure on them grows. Is this singing akin to the harmony of the spheres in its other-worldliness, the divine acknowledgement of the immanent miracle? Or is it, as Roger believes, merely the first sign of an impending disaster? Then there is the pit at the crossways. Anyone who has read Golding's autobiographical fragment 'The Ladder and the Tree' will recognise this as the cellar of his boyhood home, fronting the graveyard and seen with an imagination imbued with Poe's *Tales of Mystery and Imagination,* just as they will recognise the spire as the tree into which the same boy escaped.[3] Yet, like the spire, the pit evokes no simple response. In terms of the physical analogy, it would represent the bowels, the centre of corruption and the darkness of man's heart. Psychologically, it is the Id, terrifyingly suggesting monstrous passions, barely controlled beneath the surface:

> Some form of life; that which ought not to be seen or touched, the darkness under the earth, turning, seething, coming to the boil.

On the other hand, it is ritually prepared 'like a grave made ready for some notable', and to penetrate the significance of that phrase in terms of the myth relating to Pangall, is to recognise that its terrors are compensated by its mystic power to heal and renew.

Faced with such a welter of contradictory implications and indications, one would expect the resolution to be uneasily poised on a fine balance of uncertainty, and, for much of the final section of the book, so it is. The autumn storms come, the spire groans and trembles, the masonry begins to crumble and pieces of stone fly off as if heralding the approaching apocalypse. But the spire still stands, though now out of true, enigmatically testifying to both the truth and the falsehood of the positions held by Jocelin and Roger, and apparently verifying the general truth of Father Adam's statement that 'life itself is a rickety building.' According to this reckoning, the book seems to be recreating the basic dilemma of the final paragraph of *Free Fall*, where the damp floorcloth in the prison cell had stood for the impossibility of ever really knowing.

Three incidents, however, clearly direct the reader beyond this simple solution. The first is connected with the nail referred to earlier which has been brought by the Visitor as the Church's gift to the new construction. Jocelin has always planned that this nail shall be driven in at the base of the cross right at the top of the spire; but when the nail arrives, he is much too busy trying to explain his actions to the Visitor to give it much thought. It is only when the storms are lashing the cathedral and threatening the spire, and when the people are convinced that 'Satan is loose', that Jocelin suddenly realises the immense significance of the nail in what he is doing:

> For want of a nail the shoe was lost,
> For want of a shoe the horse was lost,
> For want of a horse the rider was lost,
> For want of a rider the kingdom was lost,
> And all for the want of a horseshoe nail.

The nail, itself a symbol of the cost of man's salvation, is the very cornerstone of the miracle on which he is staking his life in his wild game with the devil. This realisation drives him through the deserted church with the devils battering at the windows, makes him seize the nail from the altar and scramble up the precarious ladders into the tip of the spire. And when Jocelin drives in the nail at the top of the spire, it is no empty piece of mumbo jumbo, no superstitious reliance on the power of the nail to avert disaster, but a positive and, in terms of the spire's construction, entirely logical act. He is nailing the cathedral to the sky in affirmation of the supremacy of his Faith over Roger's Reason. He uses the nail not because it is a conventional relic but because it epitomises the power of Faith. The nail is Jocelin's equivalent of Roger's steel hoop – not a physical stay but a spiritual one.

Yet even this affirmation is not enough to counter the terror of Jocelin's gradual awakening: he has learned that the spire was built over a murdered man by a gang of heathens, that it was bought with offices and money in the gift of his aunt, who won them as payment for her sexual services to the old king. Shortly afterwards a further stage in his progressive disillusion takes place. As Jocelin labours in great stress of soul, the dumb mason who, throughout the book, is presented as the only man who really knows Jocelin, comes to him and gestures to him to follow:

> Then the dumb man led them on tiptoe to the south east pillar and showed them where he had chiselled a little hole in the stone, then went away again on tiptoe. Jocelin understood what he had to do. He took the chisel with its burred-over head out of the hole, lifted up an iron probe and thrust it in. It sank in, in, through the stone skin, grated and pierced in among the rubble with which the giants who had been on the earth in those days had filled the heart of the pillar.

The revelation that comes to Jocelin is the huge, ironic realisation that his faith had never been big enough, that he had always based his 'miracle', and Roger his intricate calculations, on the assumption that the pillars were solid; now he discovers that they are nothing but stone skins filled with rubble, a lasting witness to the real faith of the 'giants of old' who built on mud, supported their roofs on slender shells and accepted miracles as naturally as they accepted rain from heaven. In acknowledgement Jocelin prostrates himself on the stones of the crossways as violently as he had done once before, when his first vision of the spire had come to him and the angel had first warmed his back:

> Then all things came together. His spirit threw itself down an interior gulf, down, throw away, offer, destroy utterly, build me in with the rest of them; and as he did this he threw his physical body down too, knees, face, chest, smashing on the stone.

But this time no comfort comes, for this fresh illumination has revealed to Jocelin only his own unworthiness, and he accepts the judgement that the angel-devil at his back metes out as the necessary and warranted penalty of his great presumption:

> Then his angel put away the two wings from the cloven hoof and struck him from arse to the head with a whitehot flail . . . Jocelin . . . knew that at last one good prayer had been answered.

There remains, however, one further insight for Jocelin, and this is to be the decisive one. Seeking to extract some certainty from the mess, Jocelin crawls from his sick bed and drags his decaying body down to the village, ostensibly to ask for Roger Mason's forgiveness, but really to seek the answer to the only question that is still meaningful to him – what is holding the spire up? As he leaves by the back door, he is suddenly aware of an appletree in full blossom over his head:

> He twisted his neck and looked up sideways. There was a cloud of angels flashing in the sunlight, they were pink

and gold and white; and they were uttering this sweet scent for joy of the light and the air. They brought with them a scatter of clear leaves, and among the leaves a long, black springing thing. His head swam with the angels, and suddenly he understood there was more to the appletree than one branch. It was there beyond the wall, bursting up with cloud and scatter, laying hold of the earth and the air, a fountain, a marvel, an appletree;

No sooner has this vision faded than it is immediately replaced by another, that of the kingfisher in flight across the water:

Then, where the yard of the deanery came to the river and trees lay over the sliding water, he saw all the blue of the sky condensed to a winged sapphire, that flashed once.
He cried out.
'Come back!'
But the bird was gone, an arrow shot once. It will never come back, he thought, not if I sat here all day. He began to play with the thought that the bird might return, to sit on a post only a few yards away in all its splendour, but his heart knew better.
'No kingfisher will return for me.'
All the same, he said to himself, I was lucky to see it.

At the time, the juxtaposition of these two images of evanescent light and splendour mean no more to Jocelin than a type of romantic distraction that experience has taught him to suspect:

Father Adam was right. I make too much fuss among the appletrees and the kingfishers.

It is only on his death-bed that the last insight is granted to

Jocelin to see them not as distractions but as symbols of the final truth of his original vision and of the certainty he has been seeking. For the kingfisher is the once-in-a-lifetime bird, never returning, never resting, revealing itself in all its beauty only in a flash of magic at the water's edge; and the appletree's glory, though sustained by so many branches, lasts only for a few spring days, routed by the first winds of May and lost in the wastes of the surrounding year. What these visionary gleams signify for Jocelin in terms of the spire he has built is, in effect, a final vindication of the rightness of his purpose, a vindication (in Golding's phrase) of the 'My Godness' in man that comes and goes as quickly as the kingfisher and the blossom of spring, as opposed to the terrifying, hardened, broken-down criminality in man that constantly threatens but can never quite destroy him. And it is this final certainty that penetrates the rigmarole of the last rites and brings Jocelin in the end the peace that passeth understanding, and his own form of beatitude:

What is terror and joy, how should they be mixed, why are they the same, the flashing, the flying through the panicshot darkness like a bluebird over water? . . .

In the tide, flying like a bluebird, struggling, shouting, screaming to leave behind the words of magic and incomprehension –

It's like the appletree!

But this, in a sense, is only half the story, and what remains is bound up with a character who seems at first to have nothing more than a minor part to play. Indeed, the true significance of the part that Pangall plays is revealed to all but the most discerning reader only in the last few pages of the book, when Jocelin, in his last desperate effort to find out why the spire is still standing, confronts Roger Mason with the knowledge of what has really happened to his caretaker:

What holds it up, Roger? I? The nail? Does she, or do you? Or is it poor Pangall, crouched beneath the cross-ways, with a sliver of mistletoe between his ribs?

The revelation that Pangall is in fact buried in the pit at the crossways and has not merely fled from the persecution of the workmen is enough in itself to send the hasty reader scuttling back through the novel to find out how he got there in the first place. In doing so, he discovers that Golding has carefully supplied all the necessary clues to Jocelin's discovery, without making it explicit in so many words.

The key lies in the mistletoe berry that Jocelin notices near the crossways after Pangall has apparently been hunted from the cathedral by the workmen. Its significance suddenly dawns on him when, alone on top of the spire on Midsummer Night, he sees the bale fires burning on the hills in the direction of Stonehenge and realises that Pangall has been the victim of a pagan ceremony to ward off the bad luck that the workmen feel must inevitably result from building so high and at such cost:

> he sat gazing drearily over the rim to where the bale fires leapt.
> Slowly his mind came back to its own life. If David could not build the temple because he had blood on his hands, what is to be said of us, and of me? Then the terrible christening leapt into his eye and he cried out; and then, just when he had put it away again, a host of memories flew together. He watched, powerless to stop as they added to each other. They were like sentences from a story, which though they left great gaps, still told enough. It was a story of her and Roger and Rachel and Pangall and the men. He was staring down – down past the ladders, the floors of wood, the vaulting, down to a pit dug at the crossways like a grave made ready for some notable. The disregarded bale fires shuddered round the

horizon, but there was ice on his skin. He was remembering himself watching the floor down there, where among
the dust and rubble a twig with a brown, obscene berry
lay against his foot.

He whispered the word in the high, dark air.

'Mistletoe!'

The fate of Pangall, dead like a witch at the crossroads with
a stake through the heart, is not, however, just another cross
that Jocelin has to bear, nor must Pangall be too closely
identified as the victim of a witch hunt, though the broom
which is his badge of office encourages such an interpretation.
More important is the significance that Jocelin attaches to the
incident: the pit, after all, is not described as a grave prepared
for a victim but for 'some notable', and it is Jocelin himself
who wonders whether the spire still stands as much because of
Pangall as of anything else. All of which leads one to question
the role that Pangall plays in the novel. Scapegoat he certainly
is, and even his deformity, according to Sir James Frazer (on
whose work Golding has drawn for the main myth associated
with Pangall) is one of the common characteristics of the
tainted wether of the flock who must bear the sins of the many
that all may live. That he is an outcast is stressed right from
the beginning:

> Pangall shook his head with such solemnity and cer-
> tainty, that Jocelin fell silent, looking down, mouth open.
> Pangall grounded the handle of his broom, and stood
> with his weight on it. He looked round the pavement,
> then up at the dean's face.
>
> 'One day, they will kill me.'
>
> For a while they were both silent, among the singing
> that the echo made of the work noises. The dust danced
> in the sun between them. All at once Jocelin remembered
> his joy. He dropped both his hands on the man's leather
> shoulders and gripped tight.

'They shan't kill you. No one shall kill you.'
'Then they will drive me out.'

But scapegoats are also commonly associated with the idea
of divinity: both Pangall's name and many of his physical
characteristics (e.g. his deformity and his impotency) reflect
details documented by Frazer concerning those gods who
figure as scapegoats in vegetation myths:

> Hence the Arcadian custom of whipping the image of
> Pan with squills at a festival, or whenever the hunters
> returned empty-handed, must have been meant, not to
> punish the god, but to purify him from the harmful
> influences which were impeding him in the exercise of his
> divine functions as a god who should supply the hunter
> with game. Similarly, the object of beating the human
> scapegoat on the genital organs with squills and so on
> must have been to release his reproductive energies from
> any malignant agency; and as the Thargelia at which he
> was sacrificed was an early harvest festival celebrated in
> May, we must recognise in him a representative of the
> creative and fertilising god of vegetation.

Just as the elements in myths from various different ages and
cultures cross and re-cross, so when it comes to identifying
Pangall in Golding's scheme, it is possible to trace characteristics of various gods. There is, for instance, a strong hint of the
Roman god Vulcan who was deformed and lame, while the
adultery between Pangall's wife Goody and Roger Mason,
which takes place in the 'swallow's nest' high in the golden net
of criss-cross beams, re-enacts the classical situation of Venus
and Mars trapped in the golden net of Vulcan's forging.
   But the main myth connected with Pangall is undoubtedly
that of the Norse god, Balder. Balder, according to the myth,
was rendered invulnerable to all physical hurt by the goddess
Frigg, who made all things on earth and in heaven swear not

to harm him. Then Loki, the mischief-maker, discovered that the mistletoe had not taken the oath because, rooted as it was in the oak tree itself, it was neither in heaven nor on earth. Loki used this information to bring about Balder's death – he fashioned an arrow from the mistletoe and encouraged the blind god, Hother, to shoot it at Balder. A whole complex of suggestions link this myth with Pangall: there is his death by the mistletoe, of course, but there is also the whole process by which Pangall is associated, through his ancestors who built the original church, with the very oak out of which the beams were made. According to the Balder myth, the life of the god was in the tree, a fact which was made manifest by the mistletoe itself, the golden bough which even when the tree seemed dead in winter still gave sign (the mistletoe being evergreen) of the sacred presence. The mistletoe once pulled, the god would die; or, to put it in less religious terms, no oak could be truly seasoned (or dead) while the mistletoe lived on it. It is this that causes Jocelin, when he first scrapes his foot against the mistletoe at the crossways, to have fears about the nature of the oak which is to form the octagonal framework of the spire:

> He scuffed his foot irritably; and as now so often seemed to happen, the berry and the twig could not be forgotten, but set off a whole train of memories and worries and associations which were altogether random. He found himself thinking of the ship that was built of timber so unseasoned, a twig in her hold put out one green leaf. He had an instant vision of the spire warping and branching and sprouting; and the terror of that had him on his feet. I must learn about wood, he thought, and see that every inch of it is seasoned.

The apparently 'random' link between pagan myths of the oak on the one hand and its building properties on the other might at the simplest level reflect the differing points of view of

the workmen and of Jocelin, of pagan superstition set against
Christian enlightenment; but the use of the Balder myth in
connection with the persecution and death of Pangall prepares
one for a further interpretation. For if Pangall is to be seen as
Balder, it is equally relevant to see Jocelin as Loki, the mischief-
maker who brings about the conditions when play (i.e. the
original treatment of Pangall by the workmen, described by
Roger as a 'joke' – just as, in the myth, the crowd amuses itself
by testing Balder's invulnerability) becomes real earnest, and
disaster follows. Read in this light, the first encounter between
Jocelin and Pangall takes on a new meaning:

> 'My great-great-grandfather helped to build it. In the
> hot weather he would roam through the roof over the
> vault up there, as I do. Why?'
> 'Softly, Pangall, softly!'
> 'Why? Why?'
> 'Tell me then.'
> 'He found one of the oak logs smouldering. By the luck
> of his wit he carried an adze with him. If he went for
> water the roof would have been ablaze and the lead like a
> river before he could get back. He adzed out the embers.
> He made a hole you could hide a, a child in; and he
> carried the embers out in arms that were roasted like
> pork. Did you know that?'
> 'No.'
> 'But I know it. We know it. All this – ' And he made a
> jab with his broom at the dust-laden moulding – 'this
> breaking and digging up – let me take you into the roof.'
> 'I've other things to do and so have you.'
> 'I must speak with you –'
> 'And what d'you suppose you're doing now?'
> Pangall took a step back. He looked round at the
> pillars and the high, glittering windows as if they could
> tell him what to say.
> 'Reverend Father. In the roof. Just by the door from

the stair in the south-west turret there is an adze, shar-
pened, tallowed, guarded, ready.'

'That's well done. Wise.'

Pangall made a gesture with his free hand.

'It's nothing. It's what we are for. We've swept,
cleaned, plastered, cut stone and sometimes glass, we've
said nothing –'

'You've all been faithful servants of the House. I try to
be one myself.'

'My father, and my father's father. And the more so
since I'm the last.'

'She's a good woman and wife, my son. Hope and be
patient.'

'They've made a game of my whole life. And more. It's
not just this – Come and see my cottage.'

'I've seen it.'

'But not in the last few weeks. Come quickly –' and
limping, hurrying with a beckoning hand, his broom
trailing from the other, Pangall led the way into the
south transept. 'It was our place. What will become of
us?'

As long as Pangall is seen as nothing more than an old
caretaker, tired of the disturbance of his settled life, resenting
the dirt and the profanity of the workmen, his words sound
like a typical complaint against the brave new world by a
typical representative of the old. But if Pangall is linked with
Balder, then other questions arise. What is meant by his being
the last of an unbroken line going back to his great-great-
grandfather and the earliest foundation of the church? What is
the 'kingdom' he is being driven out of? What home is he
losing? The answers to these questions may have something to
do with Golding's sense of the proximity of those two great
religious monuments, one pagan (Stonehenge) and one
Christian (Old Sarum) which were part of medieval Salisbury. The 'giants of old', their line now reduced to one impo-

tent lame man, were not themselves pagan for they built a
Christian church, but they built at a time when such distinctions had little real meaning, when the religious impulse
lacked the sophistication to discriminate nicely between
Christ and Balder, but prompted men nevertheless to take the
biggest of all dares and to erect impossible buildings, under
impossible conditions, in impossible places.

What Pangall's kingdom stands for, then, is something very
similar to what the Neanderthals' kingdom stood for in *The
Inheritors* – a state of religious innocence pre-dating what
might be called theological man, its loss as much to be regretted as was that other kingdom. As much to be regretted, yet,
as in *The Inheritors*, as much to be accepted; for if the incident
of Jocelin's terror at the thought of what will happen to the
spire if the wood is not seasoned has meaning at all, the
meaning must be that it is *necessary* for the evergreen god to
die, in fact as in symbol. We can no longer rely exclusively on
the readiness of the adze and the vigilance of men: we must all
'learn about wood'.

Pangall's ancient yet precarious kingdom, the cottage that
hangs beneath the shelter of the cathedral wall, has been built,
like each successive culture, out of the rubble left by its
predecessors, 'loot turned up in some cold harbour that the
Romans had not seen for a thousand years.' Golding has
subsequently pointed out that Cold Harbour was a name
given by Saxon wayfarers to the Roman ruins they used as
shelters.[4] But the cottage is surrounded by 'the piles of
building materials that crowded round it, one insolence
attacking another', the insolence of ancient rights and
privileges challenged by the pride and mastery of the new
order. Just as the Roman materials, after the fall of Rome, are
incorporated into his cottage, so Pangall is himself horribly
incorporated into the building of the new spire whose advent
he had resisted, pegged against the shifting earth that holds it
up so miraculously. And the mistletoe sprig that holds Pangall
to the earth is the pagan equivalent of the nail that pierced

Christ, sacrificed for man's salvation, the nail that holds the straining spire to the sky, as Jocelin believes. Jocelin too falls, not under the blows of the builders, but beneath the flail of the ambiguous angel with the cloven hoof. His body with its decaying spine is associated with the spire itself, standing impossibly on its hollow pillars. Jocelin, like Pangall, becomes a hunted man, outcast and victim, but the murderous townspeople spare him when they see that sickness has already taken its toll of his body. Moments before his death, Jocelin has an extraordinary vision of man's physical fragility, his vulnerability:

> He saw all people naked, creatures of light brown parchment, which bound in their pipes or struts. He saw them pace or prance in sheets of woven stuff, with the skins of dead animals under their feet . . .

His alienated perception sees the dance of death, the body's transience.

Yet the final vision is, after all, that of kingfisher and appletree, become one with the created and permanent beauty of the spire Jocelin has built, at the cost of four lives, and out of the death agonies of Pangall and Goody, and the life-in-death paralysis of Roger Mason. Golding himself should have the final word:

> If the reader, the critic does not understand that after all the theology, the ingenuities of craft, the failures and the sacrifices, a man is overthrown by the descent into his world of beauty's mystery and irradiation, flame, explosion, then the book has failed.

2

The Pyramid
(1967)

'Faced by the white blank page,' the artist, according to
Golding, 'creates . . . a calculation and balance, an engineering job of girders and interlocking forces'.[1] The result of such
building might (metaphorically speaking) be a spire or a
pyramid – both massive, upward-pointing man-made con-
structions. Yet in obvious ways these two novels seem contrasted or counterpointed, their differences being more apparent than their similarities. The fourteenth-century setting of
The Spire is exchanged for the present century; the artist's
vision for the adolescent's self-absorption; an uninterrupted
sequence of events for three separate episodes; a mood of
relentless intensity, even tragedy for one of social comedy,
even farce. *The Pyramid* is undoubtedly one of Golding's fun-
niest books, sometimes hilariously so, displaying not only a
pointed verbal wit but a delight in the comic potential of
awkward situations; in this as in some other respects it lies
much closer to the mainstream of the English novel than any
of his earlier work. Deliberately, it seems, Golding here
retracts his scope from the wider horizons of his earlier books
(after the bomb, before history) to focus on English provincial
life. The theme of a young man growing up in a narrow-
minded, tight-laced society, rebelling against its prejudices yet
unconsciously sharing them, traditionally provides oppor-
tunities for humour and social criticism. Golding exposes the

underside of his small town life as shrewdly as *Clochemerle* exposed its French equivalent, or as Kingsley Amis exposed the pretensions of academe in *Lucky Jim*. Further differences from the preceding novel are apparent at a linguistic level: in *The Spire* language is consistently dense and at times convoluted or congested, heightened and enriched with symbolic or poetic resonances; that of *The Pyramid* was intended to be 'limpidly' simple (in Golding's phrase),[2] prosaic and limited. Musical and dramatic metaphors occur but in general the resources of language are deliberately cut back in order to reflect more exactly the depleted inner life of Stilbourne society which tends to foster misunderstandings; at times these are occasioned by the widespread use of euphemisms. Such misunderstandings are part of a more fundamental breakdown in communication resulting from a number of individual failures to love or listen with full attention.

Geographically, of course, the spire of Barchester/Salisbury and the square of Stilbourne/Marlborough are no great distance from one another. When Jocelin looks out north-east from his spire, he sees with the foreshortening eye of the imagination 'the white stones of the new bridge at Stilbury, . . . the very nuns, or two of them at least, in their garth, though they were enclosed, and this distant inspection a breaking of the wall'. Figures crossing over the new bridge remind him that it is market day at Stilbury, though not in the city. In *The Pyramid*, five hundred years later, Stilbury has become, more tellingly, Stilbourne, but it is still a market town. The new bridge has become the Old Bridge, but it still carries the main traffic southward to Barchester; the square-based society of Stilbourne, still as enclosed as the convent had been, nevertheless gravitates towards the city for occasions such as Imogen Grantley's cathedral wedding.

'For most of my life, childhood, boyhood and more, we lived at Marlborough. Our house was on the Green, that close-like square, tilted south with the Swindon road running through it' Golding related in his fragment of an autobiography, 'The

Ladder and the Tree'.[3] Stilbourne is recognisably Marlborough, cut down in size perhaps but with most of its land-
marks still identifiable – the close-like Green, the High Street
and the Town Hall down whose steps Lily, his nurse, led the
infant Golding of 'Billy the Kid', as she took him to school for
the first time.[4] Marlborough is a tight little enclave, wedged
between Savernake Forest to the south, the downs to the
north, and crossed by the river Kennet, flowing from west to
east, where Marlborough College stands on its banks. In *The
Pyramid*, Evie's father has warned her against going south into
the woods after dark, and there are further dangers lurking to
east and west: Oliver finds himself 'envisaging Stilbourne with
college gents to the east, stable lads to the west, a spread of
hot, sexy woodland to the south of it and only the bare
escarpment to the north'. As if to emphasise Stilbourne's
repressions, Golding surrounds the town with place names
redolent of Oliver's developing sexuality: to the west, 'Hotton
where the racing stables were', reachable 'by way of Cockers';
eastward along the river is the unnamed College and the steep
Pillicock; to the south lies the vulgar-sounding Bumstead
(modified, perhaps, by the clerical epithet 'Episcopi'), the
woods and the equally earthy Leg O'Mutton pond; north-
wards, like a body stretched out, is the bare escarpment with
its suggestively 'furry' clump, site of the first of the novel's two
acts of exposure.

Oliver and his mother and father (significantly the only
family in Stilbourne not to be given a surname) resemble
Golding's own family in several respects, though unlike
Oliver, Golding shared their attention with a younger brother.
Like their counterparts in *The Pyramid*, his parents were both
skilled amateur musicians, his mother playing the piano, his
father the violin; both were lovingly concerned with their son's
welfare while finding it difficult to understand him or answer
his deepest needs. They occupied an uneasy and indeterminate place in the class pyramid whose existence, so central to
the book's tensions, has always distressed Golding:

My father was a master at the local grammar school so that we were all the poorer for our respectability. In the dreadful English scheme of things at that time, a scheme which so accepted social snobbery as to elevate it to an instinct, we had our subtle place . . . like everybody except the very high and the very low in those days, we walked a social tightrope.

As for Oliver, he is at times a little reminiscent of his author – on the small side but chunky and combative (as 'Billy the Kid' had indicated[6]), a good pianist, noted rather for his *sforzando* than his *diminuendo*. Even his Oxford college sounds like Golding's own Brasenose, with 'the spire of the University Church stretching above'.

Yet despite the presence of these autobiographical, and thus to some extent incidental elements, little in the planning of *The Pyramid* seems to have been left to chance. Indeed it is difficult to imagine that Golding, for whom Egypt had so long had an 'inward connection' and fascination, whose favourite period of history was 'the Egypt of mystery, of the pyramids and the valley of the Kings'[7] would have used such a title and an epigraph drawn from the Instructions of Ptah Hotep, without intending them to have some special significance. Marlborough was chosen as the setting, not merely because Golding knew it from the inside but because it had certain social characteristics and geographical features which made it especially appropriate to his purpose: the most important of these being the Green/Square. The Square forms the base of the pyramid. The fictional town is called Stilbourne both because it suggests resistance to change, stagnant water, death at birth, unrealised possibilities, for without the quickening power of love, the book's various relationships are doomed to be stillborn. A pyramid is dedicated to the preservation of an embalmed corpse, to perpetuating a way of death. Such a tomb is made for the highest by the lowest and is thus the product of a rigid social hierarchy.

The sense of entrapment, of being caught within the stale air of the tomb of the living dead is passionately voiced by Oliver at the moment of his own greatest disillusionment:

> 'Life can't – I mean just out there, you have only to look up at the sky – but Stilbourne accepts it as a *roof*. As a – and the way we hide our bodies, and the things we don't say, the things we daren't mention, the people we don't meet – and that *stuff* they call music – it's a lie! Don't they understand? It's a lie, a lie! It's – obscene!'

In denouncing the town's narrow-mindedness, Oliver focuses particularly on its hypocritical attitudes towards sex, class and music, the book's three main concerns. Structurally, if the square forms the base of the novel's pyramid, then the sides must be triangular surfaces, and each of these topics can be presented as three-sided. Class can be divided into upper, lower and middle (though all are aspects of the middle-class itself – the book is not concerned with the real upper classes or the unemployed); attitudes to sex may be divided into repressive, sublimating or idealising (Oliver's crush on Imogen) and lustful (his desire for Evie). Music too can be divided into jazz, the sexy music of the Savoy Hotel Orpheans which Evie listens to every night on the wireless, but Oliver hates; classical music, which is Oliver's passion, and between these two the nondescript and lifeless music of the musical comedy, *The King of Hearts*, the Ivor Novelloish piece performed by the Stilbourne Operatic Society (whose initials pointedly spell SOS – also an acronym for 'Save Our Souls'). A diagram could be constructed of triangular motifs based on the square, together forming a pyramid, though the fourth side is less readily identifiable: it might equally well be represented by the three sections of the novel, its three main characters or even the three aspects of man. Golding, defending the book's triadic structure in a recent interview, explained 'We all have three elements.'[8] A diagram of it seen in these terms, might

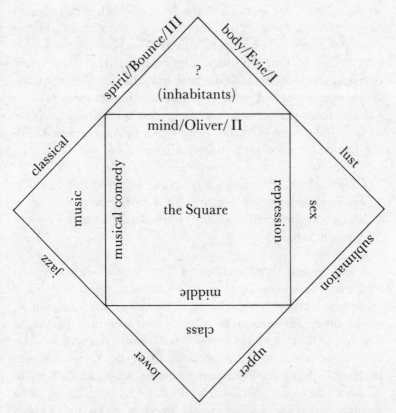

Figure 1 The triadic structure of *The Pyramid*

look something like figure 1.

Set out in this way, the book's structure seems implausibly schematic. Triadic groupings are nevertheless evident throughout, with characters regularly tending to fall into triangular relationships: Oliver, Robert, Evie; Oliver, Evie, Imogen; Oliver and his mother and father; Oliver, Henry, Bounce; or Bounce, Henry and Mary Williams. There are no 'eternal triangles', though Oliver, in confusion and perhaps with unconscious irony, thinks of himself as having 'cuck-olded' Sergeant Babbacombe after he has made love to Evie ('I was a bit vague about cuckolding, but it seemed the right

word'). The three sections of the book, though very different
in tone, have a complex and interlocking relationship which is
clearly the product of considerable skill and craftsmanship, as
well as insight. One point that does emerge in the construction
of triangular motifs is that the base line, the line of the Square,
is always associated with the middle, the compromise position, lukewarm between the energising qualities of physical
or spiritual, hot or cold. With the writer of Apocalypse, Golding has no time for such indeterminate states:

> I know thy works, that thou art neither cold nor hot: I
> would thou wert cold or hot. So then because thou art
> lukewarm and neither cold nor hot, I will spue thee out
> of my mouth.

The first and third sections of *The Pyramid* are concerned
with two women who, in their different ways, reject Stilbourne
and elude its dead hand by escaping – in one case to London,
in the other, into madness. The middle section, however, is
devoted to the drama of the town itself and in particular to the
farcical activities of the Stilbourne Operatic Society. Something of Golding's unobtrusive craftsmanship can be seen in
his handling of this section. The book, he has explained, has a
musical structure, appropriately enough given its concern
with music: it is based on a sonata form, with the middle
section as a scherzo, or light-hearted joke.[9] Seen thus, the
bridging middle section not only works well but, as in music,
is firmly related to what has gone before and what is to come
afterwards. The connecting link is Oliver's growing awareness, through the sheer puerility of the operetta *The King of
Hearts*, of the emptiness that lies behind the social life and
values of the Square, and further, behind the 'sacred beauty'
and sweet smile of his idealised love, the upper middle-class
Imogen Grantley. This recognition is brought about by one of
Golding's most successful comic characters, the producer of
the operetta, Evelyn de Tracy: 'She's a stupid, insensitive,

vain woman, she has a neat face and just enough sense to keep smiling' is how he describes Imogen. In doing so, he fulfils his promise to cure Oliver of the boyish infatuation which was so obvious to him, though not – apparently – to anyone else. Plain speaking of this kind is very different from the earlier flattery, so exaggerated as to seem deliberately ironic, with which he had soothed the ruffled feathers of the performers. In his role as producer, de Tracy had seemed totally unconscious of the absurdity of what he later refers to as 'this outrageous exercise in bucolic ineptitude'. In one respect, he can be seen as the typical jobbing professional, the common man's view of the theatrical 'artiste', scraping a living simply by being charmingly obsequious, eccentrically dressed and speaking in tones that are 'beautifully clear and gentle'.

But he is not entirely the self-effacing and supportive figure he seems. There is a more sinister side to him which is partly suggested by his name: 'Evelyn de Tracy' does not merely sound effeminate and affected, it also invites us to transpose it to make 'a trace of evil' or possibly 'a trace of Eve'. He explains to Oliver that he understands Imogen because 'I have a great deal of woman in me,' a fact which Oliver is disastrously unable to comprehend. Names are often carefully chosen in Golding's novels, and as well as Evelyn's, there is Evie, a corruption (even a fall from innocence?) of Eve. Oliver's name has the necessary letters to suggest a complex nature, capable of becoming 'vile' or 'evil', but one that can also 'live' or 'love'. Evelyn's honeyed talk and his effeminacy may be intended to suggest the tempting serpent (often portrayed with a woman's face in medieval illustrations of the fall). There is certainly something reptilian about his strange eyes with their minute pupils and irises invaded by yellow flakes and crystals, his sinuous movements, even perhaps in his final departure, curled up like a serpent on the seat of the bus to Barchester. His thinning hair stands up on his head like a horn, and it may be that he plays the part of a minor devil, exposing and encouraging all the pettiness, jealousies and snobbery of Stilbourne. He could be a comic devil in the vein of C.S. Lewis's *Screwtape Letters,* or a version of Mephistopheles, as he brings Oliver firmly up against unwelcome truths.

The importance of the second section is that it presents, in their most debased and caricatured form, the three themes – class, love (or sex) and music – which make up the 'crystal pyramid' to which Stilbourne 'vibrated in time'. The only explanation that Evelyn can offer in response to Oliver's insistent questioning is that life is 'an outrageous farce . . . with an incompetent producer', in fact a mirror image of *The King of Hearts* itself, where class differences have degenerated to a ludicrous argument between a conceited newspaper owner who wants, in his stage role, to address the reluctant Oliver as 'My man', while Oliver's mother passionately insists upon 'General', and finally agrees to the compromise position of 'Captain'; where love is reduced to the empty gestures of cardboard characters in a cardboard world, and where music is no more than tinklingly pretty tunes sung by effete and bloodless amateurs in thin and reedy voices.

The urge to perform which sporadically brings the Stilbourne Operatic Society to life is itself an acknowledgement of a need to enact those very passions and commitments which the society as a whole is engaged in repressing or disguising. Ironically the hollow theatrical emotions promote all sorts of offstage quarrels, releasing inhibitions and revealing the tensions that lie so near the surface of the delicate social pyramid:

> With diabolical inevitability, the very desires to act and be passionate, to show off and impress, brought to full flower the jealousies and hatreds, meannesses and indignations we were forced to conceal in ordinary life.

For Oliver the absurdity of the production in which he is obliged to play an unwilling role, stooping for coins and saluting the hero, brings home to him the theatricality of

Stilbourne life. He is linked to Evelyn de Tracy in being an unwilling participant in what they both recognise as a farce. The large gin that Evelyn buys him as the only consolation he can offer for the dire fate of living in Stilbourne *does* liberate Oliver, not only to voice the book's most outspoken criticism of Stilbourne's hypocrisy, but to make a further demand: 'Evelyn, I want the *truth* of things.' De Tracy's response is to offer him an image which is at once another kind of play-acting and yet, at least for Evelyn, an instance of truth itself. It is a series of photographs of himself dressed as a ballerina, in some of which he is supported by a heavy young man. In response to these, all Oliver's sophistication vanishes, and his helpless laughter reveals him as the country bumpkin once more. The truth of Evelyn's transvestism is too bizarre for him to grasp. The producer hastily takes back his pictures, explaining that they too were 'Just a farce', and when Oliver tries to restore the conversation to its former intimacy, inviting Evelyn to speak of truth and honesty once more, he replies evasively 'It escapes me, I'm afraid.' This section, like the first, ends with the achievement of one insight and the loss of another. Oliver passes some psychic ear-tests and fails others. He responds to problems that lie wholly outside his experience with incomprehension and, because this movement is a scherzo, with a naive and dismissive laughter.

Of the three main themes – class, love, and music – class is the one that, for Golding, was most likely to have provided the *raison d'être* of the novel. In an interview with W.L. Webb of *The Guardian,* given after the publication of *Rites of Passage,* Golding agreed that the influence of the 'ghastly' social structure of his childhood had been underestimated in his work:[10]

It was about as stratified a society as you could well find anywhere in the country, and I think that the pyramidal structure of English society is present, and my awareness of it is indelibly imprinted in me, in my psyche, not merely in my intellect but very much in my emotional,

almost my physical being. I am enraged by it and I am
unable to escape it entirely, though obviously as I get
older and also as I get better known I have less and less
cause to worry about whether I am middle-class, lower
middle-class, lower *lower* middle-class . . . It dissolves
but it doesn't disappear; it's fossilised in me.

'Those unbelievable gradations,' as Oliver calls them in the novel,
are starkly displayed in Stilbourne. The image of society as a
pyramid is particularly appropriate, dedicated to preserving a
corpse, yet physically a structure which is wide at the base and
narrow at the top, which can be ascended step by painful step.
Both Henry Williams and Oliver set about climbing it gradually
and they are bound by the kinship of survivors, social climbers
who are willing to pay whatever is reasonable, who have not given
themselves away as the vulnerable Evie and Bounce have done.
At the other extreme, Captain Wilmot exemplifies the dire
consequences of being too abruptly translated from one class to
another. An officer and a gentleman when his country had needed
him, in reality he is nothing more than a junior clerk, living in a
cottage similar to that of the loud and vulgar Sergeant Babbacombe; the result is a symbolic crippling of the body, and a mind
stunted and immature.

The social pyramid is necessarily fragile. The situation
Oliver fears most of all is not so much his failure to rise as the
possibility of falling, of bringing disgrace on himself and his
family. He agonises over how his parents would feel if, as a
result of his affair with Evie, she became pregnant and he was
obliged to marry her:

To be related, even if only by marriage, to *Sergeant Babbacombe*! I saw their social world, so delicately poised and
carefully maintained, so fiercely defended, crash down
into the gutter. I should drag them down and down
through those minute degrees where it was impossible to
rise but always easy to fall.

The delicate nature of social relationships has been revealed earlier when Oliver realises from the warmth of Mrs Babbacombe's smile that Evie has used him as a stalking-horse for her joy-rides with Bobby Ewan, the doctor's son, who unlike Oliver is quite outside her social range, at least in her parents' opinion. Oliver uses his discovery of her deceit to bully her, and threatening to 'tell' soon becomes a way of exerting power over her, a substitute for the primitive club.

In this class struggle only the extremes are relatively unaware of what is going on. The novel alludes to them but does not include them: at the top, the college boys simply ignore the rest of the town, while at the bottom the unemployed (the book is set in the hard times of the 1930s) lounge about outside the pubs, unable to afford to go in. In between, the gradations are subtle but, in terms of the ethos of the Square, unquestioned, depending as they do on such unequivocal attributes as profession, possessions, type of house, type of school, habits, even looks, as well as a whole series of instinctive taboos. Thus Norman and Imogen are chosen to take the leads in the operatic production not because they can act or sing but because, apart from the Mayor whose social standing is as good as theirs, everyone in the Square accepts their superior status. Norman is the owner of *The Stilbourne Advertiser* and therefore the voice of Stilbourne – it turns out to be suitably thin and 'gnat-like'. In Stilbourne's eyes, however, he is a man of importance, a man of property that includes a green, open Lagonda. If Oliver envies Norman his possession of Imogen, he envies Bobby Ewan his possession of Evie. His father is a doctor and though Bobby does not yet have his own car, he has a red motor bike instead. Oliver's father is only the doctor's dispenser, and Oliver cannot drive at all. Nor is the cliff that separates Bobby's world from that of Oliver merely a matter of professions and possessions. Bobby Ewan has been to boarding school, and is going on to Cranwell to train as an RAF officer, has a profile like the Duke of Wellington, and can fight like a boxer; Oliver goes to the local grammar school, looks like a milkman, is an HP sauce man, and fights like a lout. It is inevitable in the conflict between them that Oliver should win, but equally inevitable that he should feel shame in victory while Bobby demonstrates contempt in defeat.

Oliver, of all the characters in the novel, seems most aware of the need to climb the steps of the social pyramid, but Henry Williams, in his own quiet way, shows the most natural talent for the task. Starting from the lowest point as little more than a Welsh vagrant, he ends up owning Williams Garage, Williams Showrooms, Williams Farm Machinery, and a large piece of Stilbourne to boot; and all this apparently without losing the essential kindliness of his nature. His rise promotes envy and malicious gossip, of course, but it would not be Stilbourne if it did not; and even at the end of the story he is essentially the same warm, friendly fellow as he walks across the gleaming concrete to give Oliver, who has also hitched himself up several notches on the social scale, his personal attention (though he does not go so far as to offer him free petrol). Henry too has paid the price of success. As he admires Oliver's car, Oliver recognises that

> His attitude was typical of the deep thing lying in him, the reason for it all, tarmac, glass, concrete, machinery, the thrust not liked or enjoyed but recognised as inevitable, the god without mercy.

Deep down, Oliver knows that the 'god without mercy' that drives people to struggle up the pyramid is destructive, that the itch for success yields to no medicine. Oliver's father might think that all Oliver's problems can be solved with a dose of opening medicine, but the disease of Stilbourne is more deadly, more incapable of cure than the infection he fears Oliver may have picked up in his encounters with Evie: 'We were our own tragedy and did not know we needed catharsis.' It attacks everything and everybody within the Square, and the only possible remedy – as with the plague of old – is flight.

Three of the novel's characters recognise this and struggle to break free. Oliver and Evie do it by physically leaving the town itself, but are drawn back with the awesome fascination of felons returning to the scene of their crimes. Bounce chooses another method, and escapes first into insanity (in which she finds a strange tranquility) and finally, death; but her restless spirit survives in Stilbourne, a trapped budgerigar feebly flapping its life away against the locked windows of her empty house.

The need for escape is related to the book's second main theme expressed in the epigraph taken from the Instructions of Ptah Hotep, an ancient Egyptian sage: 'If thou be among people, make for thyself love, the beginning and end of the heart.' Golding himself has drawn attention to the different emphases that might be put on the words 'for thyself' in the phrase 'make *for thyself* love', so that it can be made to yield different meanings.[11] The disease of Stilbourne (and indeed of any class-ridden society, since, as Oliver discovers when he leaves, Stilbourne is 'like anywhere else') is its inability to follow this instruction in its nobler sense. Rather, it eats the heart out of love, leaving only the alternatives of dull respectability or illicit sex. This, in so far as such a term is appropriate to the method of Golding's later work, is the 'message' of the novel; and it is communicated with great skill through two apparently widely differing though in fact closely connected stories – those of Oliver and Evie, and of Henry and Bounce.

Golding chose for his two central women characters the names Babbacombe and Dawlish, neighbouring towns on the South Devon coast. Was this merely a random choice, or do their names hint at a kinship between these superficially highly dissimilar characters? Golding has said that he set about constructing the literary equivalent of a Beethoven sonata, in which the opening section is a statement of theme, the middle a scherzo, a light-hearted commentary on it, and the last section a series of variations on and a final resolution of that theme.[12] And so it is. The Bounce story partly reverses the story of Evie (as is indicated by Bounce's car being stuck in the woods at the *beginning* of section one, and at the *end* of section three) but it is still essentially the same story, and the two women stand in ironic counterpoint to each other throughout.

Indeed the whole of the last section works by a series of inversions. Evie is physically very attractive, exuding 'the breathlessness of perpetual sex' with her bright eyes and thick eyelashes, shoulder-length bob, cotton summer dresses, and sensual walk; Bounce is her antithesis, being of a gender 'indeterminate rather than female', having a yellow complexion, mousy hair in a bun, lashless eyes, and masculine gait and habits. Evie's overt sex appeal conceals a 'life-long struggle to be clean and sweet'. The 'erotic woods' may *seem* to be her natural habitat, she may *seem* to be 'life's necessary, unspeakable object' – 'life's lavatory', which Stilbourne accepts as long as it is safely hidden in the trees – but Evie's real longing is for openness: her revenge and triumph consist in dragging sex out into the clear light of day, insisting that Oliver have her, if he have her at all, on the bare escarpment in full view of the town on the 'saintly' Imogen Grantley's wedding day. She teaches him a further lesson when she loudly accuses him of raping her, when they are in the pub having their last drink together. Bounce, on the other hand, is a product of Stilbourne who pathetically makes her final stand against its values by demonstrating her physical needs in public, walking along the pavement 'wearing her calm smile, her hat and gloves and flat shoes – and wearing nothing else whatever'. Earlier Oliver had found her staring into the woods whose dark secrets she longs for but will never know. She is drawn, not to the light, but towards the darkness which has surrounded her since childhood and which bred such terrors in the young Oliver when he was taken by candlelight to visit the lavatory he did not want to use.

The episode of Bounce, her dark house, and the young boy who came to visit her, evokes distant echoes of Miss Haversham and Pip in *Great Expectations,* reminiscences of which had occurred earlier in the book – especially in the fight between Oliver and Bobby Ewan, which recalls that of Pip and Herbert Pocket. But it is in the final section, and particularly in the relationship between Bounce and Evie, and between Miss Haversham and Estella, that the connection seems most significant. Though the paths of these two never actually cross, they seem to be bound together with invisible bonds, sharing the same common needs and attitudes. When Evie says:

'Nobody wants me, just my damned body, not me. And I'm damned and you're damned . . . You never loved me, nobody ever loved me. I wanted to be loved, I wanted somebody to be kind to me – I wanted –'

she is searching for the real love that Oliver will not give her, any more than Henry Williams is prepared to give it to Bounce, who is left 'ludicrously pleading "All I want is for you to need me, need me!"' Oliver exploits Evie for sex, Henry exploits Bounce for her money. No wonder, when Oliver looks Henry in the eye, he sees his own face. The failure of both Oliver and Henry to love, leads both women to a wider rejection of humanity. 'She doesn't think much of people,' says Oliver's father of Evie; and Evie's hatred of Stilbourne and its inhabitants stems not merely from her painful experience that 'all men are beasts' but rather from the fact that she recognises them for the dead things they are. 'There must be *someone* . . . someone alive,' she bursts out passionately when she returns to Stilbourne after a few years in the world outside. But in her heart she knows it cannot be and that Stilbourne will be Stilbourne for as long as pyramids last. Bounce's rejection of human kind is even more comprehensive: 'D'you know, Kummer?' she says, 'If I could save a child or a budgie from a burning house, I'd save the budgie.' And there is a spine-chilling quality about her final act when she burns everything that belonged to her former life, as if ensuring that these particular funerary objects would not accompany her on her last journey: the music that was supposed, according to her father, to compensate for all earthly deprivation because 'Heaven is Music', the photograph of him, even the beautifully polished pyramid of the metronome by whose steady beat she had vainly attempted to regulate her life. The scene has something in common with the moment in *Heart of Darkness* when Kurtz scrawls across his eloquent report for the International Society for the Suppression of Savage Customs – 'Exterminate all the brutes!'

Bounce's funeral pyre of her music is in part a belated gesture of rejection of her brutal father. Accounts of his treatment of her, for her young pupil Oliver, fuse

> into a sombre picture: Crack! over the knuckles with a ruler – Bonk! in the organ loft with a roll of music – Jab! in the ribs with the point of a bow – I came to a vivid awareness of lunging Mr Dawlish with his ready hand and his eye fixed on the absolute.

Evie, like Bounce, is a victim of paternal sadism – in her case 'the sergeant's army belt with its buckle and rows of shining brass studs', whose welts Oliver has glimpsed on her thighs. The need both women feel for love may be in part a response to their fathers' cruelty and failure to cherish them rightly. For Evie, the relationship with her father, like all her dealings with men, seems to have taken a distinctly sexual turn, though this is one of the truths that Oliver cannot assimilate, and the first section leaves him brooding over Evie's reference to his 'laughing and telling . . . (about) Me 'n' Dad'. For Oliver, she has become 'this undiscovered person' with 'her curious slip of the tongue'.

Oliver, like Henry, is 'quick to feel, slow to learn' the lessons of the heart. What he learns comes too late and, in any case, the cost of further knowledge is more than he is prepared to pay; the class struggle demands too much of his attention and there is scant time for looking back. This resolution of the novel's theme is appropriately reinforced in musical terms. 'Don't be a musician, Kummer, my son,' says Bounce to Oliver. 'Go into the garage business if you want to make money.' And this, figuratively speaking, is what Oliver has done. He has the unusual advantage of 'absolute' or perfect pitch, the privilege of being native to a 'landscape where notes of music, and all sounds were visible, coloured things'. He has the ability to hear clearly, and, when he finally listens to her, to recognise the musical ignorance and incompetence of the high-born, tone-deaf Imogen. The purity of Evie's voice, on the other hand, if only he could have seen her as something other than an object of desire, might have allowed them to 'have made something, music perhaps, to take the place of the necessary, the inevitable, battle'. Indeed, Evie almost invites him to accompany her, when she says she would keep up her singing 'if I had someone to play for me.' But music remains for Oliver a 'private vice'. Even his pleasures are characteristically self-absorbed, and he is reluctant to share them. As if to push the analogy home, his first *coitus interruptus* with Evie is described as 'perilous onanism'. Oliver is not prepared to make any sacrifices and so he sells out to chemistry, success, and germ warfare. Henry, too, has the same potential – a natural musician with a 'voice . . . deft and light, like a musical instrument'; but his potential has been similarly diverted towards the accumulation of wealth, property, and respectability. As for Bounce, who has been brought up in the belief that one's eyes should always be firmly fixed on the absolute and that music should have precedence over love, class, worldly success or anything else, she, like her father before her, is a failed musician. Not that Bounce is a failure in the manner of Imogen Grantley of whom Oliver could say 'It was not just that she could not sing. It was that she was indifferent to the fact that she could not sing.' Bounce's failure is more genuinely tragic in that her whole life turns out to be based on a lie:

Bounce turned to the keyboard. She pulled a dusty and dog-eared volume out of the mess on the piano, flicked over the pages, arranged them on the music rest then · began to play. When she had finished she lit a cigarette.

'There you are. Now you know what you're up against.'

I hope she took my mutter for awe. But the truth is that I was stunned. What she had played was a Chopin Impromptu. The night before I had heard Cortot play it.

The truth was that Bounce could not play, and worse, far worse than that, was unconscious of the fact that she could not play. She knew at the end, of course, but that was when love had found her out. And the discovery was so appalling, the disintegration so great, that the words 'Heaven is Music' which Henry had inscribed on her tomb seem a bitter irony, the smile on the face of the skull.

Seen in this way, as a kind of musical elegy for lost harmonies or unresolved discords, *The Pyramid* is a deeply gloomy novel, one of the most pessimistic of all Golding's works. At the same time, there is something of a mystery about it that makes one wonder whether the pessimism that comes through might be less the result of the darkness that Golding feels surrounds man than a reflection of the novel's limitations, limitations inherent in the passion-stifling society he here records. For although, at a narrative level, *The Pyramid* works well, it leaves many unanswered questions, possibly because it does not draw on sustaining myths, as several of his other books do. Comparison with *The Spire* is revealing: the strength and effectiveness of the preceding novel, was largely due to Golding's skill in reconciling contraries and resolving, in poetic terms, the dilemma of good and evil inextricably involved in the same action. 'Was Jocelin's motive for building the spire bad or good?' seems to have been the simple question, and the equally simple response must be that no answer will entirely satisfy the mind, though Jocelin's visionary gleams may hint at a solution. Dylan Thomas, looking out over the estuary at Laugharne, and watching the sea birds with their heads in apparent supplication to heaven one minute and thrust down to kill the next, expressed this paradox in the memorable phrase 'Herons spire and spear.'

The sense of death and life mingled together, of something corrupt and yet mysteriously beautiful is only felt occasionally in this novel. It is present in Golding's picture of families that, like the Ewans, 'vibrated in time to the crystal pyramid' – an image that suggests a glass metronome, or perhaps the pulsing of the crystal that picks up radio waves, as intangible yet as real as the signals emitted by the ladies of the Square from behind the privacy of their lace curtains. It suggests something fragile, delicate, transparent (we look into it) and yet at the same time precious; but such concentrations of meaning are rare. Remembering the complexity of the pit image in *The Spire*, where the pit is figuratively both the centre of corruption and at the same time 'like a grave made ready for some notable', it is slightly disappointing that when Golding took as his central image the pyramid, something which really was 'a grave prepared for some notable', he should have made relatively little use of it. For the pyramid image affords so many promising possibilities – underground passages intended to confuse and mislead, treasure at the heart, mystery amidst corruption and death; even the outer steps, which have only appeared as the process of time (or civilisation) has worn away the original smooth surface. All or some of these aspects one might have expected to find woven into the story. Yet there is nothing in *The Pyramid* comparable to the moment when Jocelin scuffs the mistletoe with his foot and guesses the truth about Pangall, thus leading the reader towards the other myths on which Golding has drawn, even though Bounce with her car and her cats might remind one of the Egyptian goddess Bast whose (rather different) car was drawn by cats, and Evelyn de Tracy has some affinities with Set, who slew Osiris, became the Egyptian Satan and was depicted as a black serpent.

The limitations of *The Pyramid* are ultimately those of its narrator, who remains frustratingly insensitive to the events around him. Though he rails against 'the way we hide our bodies and the things we don't say, the things we daren't mention,the people we don't meet', he nevertheless fails to perceive that he has already met and rejected the taboo-breakers he thought he was looking for. Evie does and says the unmentionable before the eyes of the whole town, on the escarpment and in the pub. And though she exposes Oliver and Dr Jones (given away by a minute smear of lipstick at the corner of his mouth) it is *she* who is punished and dismissed as the scapegoat. Similarly when Bounce ignores society's invisible guidelines and takes up with the penniless Henry Williams, she is pitied as a fool, and the town closes its ranks in silent contempt, so that when Henry can finally afford to abandon her, she is left alone and friendless to sob her heart out on the hearthrug. Oliver remains in an uncomprehending ignorance of Henry's evasions and Bounce's desperations, even when he has all the evidence of her pathetic stratagems to gain Henry's attention before him; just as, in his self-absorption, he failed to comprehend the real source of Evie's problems. He cannot perceive the truth about Evie or Bounce because he has no real interest in them, never has had, and his parents' automatic assumption that he is devoted to his music teacher provides a silent critique of his failure even to like her. His wanton laughter at the words on her tomb, 'Heaven is Music' (a copybook heading as savagely ironic as the words on Evie's necklace, 'Amor vincit omnia'), shocks and revolts him, another psychic ear-test he has failed. Yet in the end it is Bounce, not Oliver or Henry Williams, who finally succeeds in repudiating Stilbourne and its values entirely. Discussing *The Scorpion God*, Golding has observed, 'Herodotus says that the Egyptians do everything in public that other people do in private.'[13] Perhaps within the stifling Stilbourne pyramid, it is Evie and Bounce who prove themselves true Egyptians, rejecting the death of the heart and struggling towards another mode of being, where love may some day conquer.

3

The Scorpion God

(1971)

Reviewing a book on man's prehistory, Golding wrote in 1961[1]

> We can see the sack of Babylon and the blasting of Hiroshima as one and the same thing, a disease endemic but not incurable. It is not too much to say that man invented war at the very earliest moment possible ... knowledge of his tragic past should render him less of a slave to the future.

He has described his fictional treatment of historical material in a recent interview: 'to some extent, I'm sending up the idea of history, and have my tongue in my cheek much more often than people suspect.'[2] Somewhere between these two extremities, tragic warning and comic send-up, *The Scorpion God* runs its course. Its three constituent stories are all set in the remote past, the first two – the title story and 'Clonk Clonk' – in prehistoric times, while the third, 'Envoy Extraordinary', is set in Imperial Rome. This last was actually written first, indeed is one of Golding's early works, having originally appeared in a volume of fantastic short stories, *Sometime, Never* (1956), with companion pieces by John Wyndham and Mervyn Peake. Golding liked it enough to rewrite it as a three-act play, *The Brass Butterfly*, which was performed in the West End in 1958 with Alastair Sim in the title role. This and 'The Scorpion God' employ the semi-didactic mode which Golding has termed 'fable'.[3] Both are concerned with the limitations, risks and actual dangers of a world view narrowly based on logic, rationalism and faith in 'scientific progress', but otherwise they have little in common. The book lacks a deliberate unity, other than its descent into 'the dark backward and abysm of time'. Assiduous analysis can always be made to yield common ground between individual works, but these three stories are concerned with distinctive societies and draw independent lessons from them.

Egypt first entered Golding's fiction somewhat obliquely in *Free Fall* where the infant Sammy was fascinated by a particular set of cigarette cards depicting Egyptian kings. His passion led him into trouble almost at once as his friend Philip persuaded him to bully the smaller boys into giving up their cards, a ploy which resulted in Philip's collection increasing, and Sammy being caught and taken to the headmaster. Much later, during the transcendent revelation that follows his experience in the cell, Sammy sees the prison camp inmates as transfigured, 'crowned with a double crown, holding in either hand the crook and flail, the power and the glory'. The portraits he draws in the light of this vision are the consummation of his art: 'those secret smuggled sketches of the haggard unshaven Kings of Egypt in their glory are the glory of my right hand and likely to remain so.' An essay 'Egypt from My Inside'[4] reveals that Sammy's obsession with the kings of Egypt was shared by his creator. At the precocious age of seven, Golding had attempted to write a play about ancient Egypt but was deterred by the thought that his characters ought to speak the appropriate language; he set himself to learn the meaning of hieroglyphics. Then followed a strange, indeed mystic encounter with the secret arcana of Egypt, apparently occasioned by a visit to the Bristol Museum.

Most sensitive children find their imaginations reluctantly seized by the fascination exerted by Egyptian mummies, 'a dead body but on permissive show behind glass'. For the small William Golding, already under the spell of things Egyptian, and subject to nightly terrors in which the corpses of the neighbouring graveyard loomed large, a mummy was a peculiarly compelling object, horrific and riveting. As he gazed at one on display in the museum, it seemed to him that a cheerful curator invited his help, and led him into an inner sanctum, where he set about unwrapping the grave-cloths from another uncoffined mummy, passing the bandages to his young assistant as he went along. Inevitably the moment came when Billy Golding stretched out his hand and touched the shrunken skin and bone of this half-wrapped embodiment of death. Curiously this incident, so vividly experienced and reported back at home and at school, took place nowhere except in his imagination, yet its reality seemed all the more intense for that. And there was a more curious sequel – in some sense a parallel, the matching half of the amulet, as it were. Golding returned to look for the cheerful curator and the room where he had helped to unwind the mummy. When he failed to find them, he went back to the showcase where his interior adventure had begun, determined to look, as if for expla-nation, into the eyes of the painted upright coffin. He clam-bered onto a chair to enable himself to do so more easily. But the eyes seemed to gaze past him, into infinity:

> It dwells with a darkness that is its light. It will not look
> at me, so frightened yet desperate, I try to force the eyes
> into mine; but know that if the eyes focused or I could
> understand the focus, I should know what it knows; and
> I should be dead.

Both the imagined experience and its real sequel point towards a single meaning, a single need that remains as strong in the adult Golding as it had been in the child – to explore the nature of death. What else could the unfinished unwinding of the grave-cloths, the passionate searching of the coffin's

painted eye signify? The Egyptians remain central to Golding's imagination because, unlike the Greeks and most modern men, they do not divorce life from death, or avert their
minds from life's only certainty, regarding any interest in it as
unwholesome or morbid. The Egyptians, like Golding, were
much possessed by death and retained their sense of its co-
existence with life: 'the heart of my Egypt therefore is to be at
once alive and dead, to suggest mysteries with no solution, to
mix the strange, the gruesome and the beautiful.'

Golding's Egypt is deeply interfused with his sense of 'a
darkness that is its light'. It gleams momentarily through
Jocelin's dying vision of men as fragile as mummies, precarious constructs of parchment and bone, or through the mysteries of *Darkness Visible*. By and large, however, this is not the
Egypt of 'The Scorpion God'. Brilliantly and convincingly
imagined though this story is, Golding's concern here seems to
be with a crucial political moment, the moment when Egyptian dynastic history began, when a king of the upper kingdom
of the Nile conquered the lower kingdom down to the delta
and estabished his capital at Memphis. Modern Egyptologists
are now sceptical as to whether exactly this sequence of events
took place at all, but the legendary conqueror is traditionally
identified as Hor-Aha, or as Narmer, and most often as Menes
(though Herodotus refers to him as 'Min').[5] A fragmentary
mace-head, now in the Ashmolean, identifies the figure of an
early king wearing the crown of the upper kingdom with a
pictograph of a scorpion – thus providing Golding with his
title. This watershed, the moment when recorded history
began, exerts something of the fascination of the moment
dramatised in *The Inheritors*, when *homo sapiens* finally defeats
the last of the Neanderthal people, and an older and stranger
order yields to a newer, more familiar one. 'The Scorpion
God' differs from the earlier novel in that it never portrays the
new order at all; its nature must be inferred from the character
of its inaugurator, though by the end of the story drastic
change is clearly imminent. On the other hand, it does share

with *The Inheritors* a quality of precise and graphic detail in the writing, so that we see everything that happens, even if we do not necessarily grasp its significance at first reading. Many of the events described have their origin in Golding's familiarity with Egyptology, though he has not striven for historical accuracy. In particular the distinctive burial practices of several different periods have been assimilated – the technologically complex embalming process would be more characteristic of later times; yet these justify their inclusion by contributing substantially to the overall atmosphere of ancient Egypt. Golding has modestly claimed that '"The Scorpion God" is Herodotus's view of Egypt more than anybody else's, it's not received archaeological opinion.'[6]

The story begins on the banks of the dried-up Nile as a kilted Egyptian king (straight from Sammy's fag cards) appears, wearing the tall white linen crown of the upper kingdom, carrying the traditional crook and flail in each hand and running heavily. He is addressed as 'Great House', a translation of the title 'Pharaoh'. For the Egyptians the king was an incarnation of the God Horus, who must prove his divine self-renewal by running a ritual race round a course called 'the field'. This represented his kingdom, just as the race represented his claim to it and his magical ability to make it fruitful. Later the course included representations of both kingdoms and was run as part of a jubilee festival at very substantial intervals, but it is thought that in archaic times the race took place more often. Golding's Great House makes his run every seven years, starting from the palace and running round the low rectangular buildings that are the houses of the dead, then back to the palace again. His success will ensure the river's rise for which all are waiting. With him, cheering and urging him on, runs the thin young man known as the Liar. There is a quality of desperation about his exhortations that reveals an underlying terror. If the God fails to complete the race and prove his potency, or if the river fails to rise high enough, the God must die. The eminent Egyptologist, W.B.

Emery, has cautiously suggested that 'It would appear probable that in primitive times, when the king showed signs of
failing powers, he was forcibly removed by death.'[7] And if the
king/God died, his household were obliged to accompany him
to the land of eternal life, to the Motionless Now that succeeds
the mere moving Now of existence. The Liar is an outsider
and does not share the calm Egyptian acceptance of death –
indeed he is simply terrified of it. Meanwhile the ten-year-old
heir to the throne explains to a blind man that his sight is
failing and that there is a kind of white smoke before his eyes –
presumably cataracts forming. The blind man steps out to
warn Great House that the prince is going blind, but just as he
does so, the God collapses, and the blind man is doubly
blamed, both for tripping him and for his evil words about the
prince – the house of God cannot be touched by sickness. The
blind man is led away to the pit, a gruesome place where
society throws its rejects and cast-offs, not so very different
from the prehistoric pit in Wiltshire that Golding described in
his essay 'Digging for Pictures'.[8]

An illicit meeting between the Liar and Princess Pretty
Flower reveals that they are lovers, though society only
appears to permit sexual relationships with kinsfolk. The Liar
urges the Princess to arouse her father, the God. At a feast
that night she dances a version of the seven veils in an effort to
seduce him, and it is clearly expected that he should make
love to her in public (according to Herodotus, the Egyptians
do in public what other people do in private).[9] But he is more
interested in playing checkers with the Head Man (presumably Herodotus's High Priest); he plays with the kind of
dicing sticks that have since been found in archaic tombs. Her
failure confirms the Head Man's view that for Great House,
this is 'a beginning' – the story amusingly reverses a number
of common phrases, so that 'private parts' become 'public
parts', and, because the Egyptians believe in an eternal life,
our phrase 'the end' becomes 'a beginning'. A mysteriously
veiled old woman brings a cup of poison. As the God's body is

elaborately prepared for burial, the river begins to rise, reaching its optimum height on the day of his formal interment in the nameless 'long, low building' round which we first saw him run. Here his mummy is placed in its three coffins, standing upright and gazing outward, the eyes and mouth open as in life. Into the tomb, singing, go all the necessary household servants and then a line of chosen representatives of the main professions, all ready to drink poison and accompany the God to his eternal kingdom – all, that is, except the Liar who refuses to die and is dismissed to the pit. The clean men (the lowest grade of priests were called 'web' i.e. 'clean' priests) seal up the tomb behind the dead and dying. The ceremonial of burial with its elaborate provision for the dead man's needs is conducted according to traditional accounts. Behind a slit stands the God's twin or double, gazing out through its stone eyes. It was believed that the soul or 'Ka' might be safely preserved within such funeral statues, though again this custom belongs more typically to the period after the unification of the kingdoms, rather than to pre-dynastic Egypt.

Alarmingly, the river continues to rise. The prince is too young, timid and effeminate to assume the mantle of the God. The Head Man, exploring the cause of the river's rise, learns of Pretty Flower's affair with the Liar and decides that he must be made to rejoin his master by force. Poison is brought and the Liar retrieved from the pit where he has ruthlessly sacrificed the blind man's life to his own survival. Cornered, he is more subversive than ever, and in the voice of a God urges Pretty Flower to make use of her army, demanding *'Supposing I were Great House?'* Such hubris is intolerable, but as the Head Man gives the order for his death, the Liar seizes one guard's spear, kills others, fatally stings the Head Man 'like a scorpion' and makes good his escape. Alone and helpless, Pretty Flower will naturally turn to her lover for guidance. What happened next is not recorded by Golding, but is evident from the archaic mace-head on which Scorpion is

depicted (see figure 2).[10] His solution to the problem of the
rising waters of the Nile was to dig artificial channels for it to
run into. At the centre of the engraved head he is shown
wearing the white crown of the upper kingdom, and holding a
hoe, while an official holds out a basket to receive the earth.
The occasion seems to be the ceremonial opening of a canal,
as he is attended by fan-bearers and slaves. Higher up, the
banners of the provinces of the north are shown, now apparently united, and from them hang the bodies of birds representing the defeated chieftains of the lower kingdom.
Obviously Scorpion had put Pretty Flower's 'beginnings of an
army' to good use, uniting the other petty chieftains along the
upper Nile beneath his rule, and then proceeding to conquer
the lower kingdom.

Herodotus, the Greek historian often thought of as the first
Egyptologist, records a comparable story, though the king's
name is different:[11]

> The priests told me that it was Min, the first king of
> Egypt, who raised the dam which protects Memphis
> from the floods . . . On the land which had been drained
> by the diversion of the river, King Min built the city
> which is now called Memphis.

Herodotus's rambling and discursive histories were sceptically received by the readers of the antique world; they
thought his stories so tall that they referred to him as 'Liar', or
more politely as 'story-teller'. It seemed to them obvious that
most of his tales simply could not be true. Herodotus, who was
by no means lacking in scepticism himself, also seems at times
to have puzzled over the causes of some of the phenomena he
recorded. One question that worried him very much (and it is
also central to 'The Scorpion God') is why the level of the Nile
rose, and why it did so at the summer solstice rather than in
late winter, like all other rivers. One explanation he was given
was that the floods were caused by snows melting from high

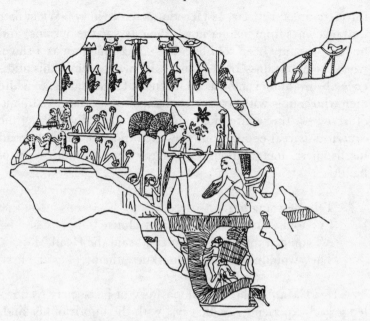

Figure 2 Scorpion King on a mace-head

mountains to the far south, near the river's source, but this seemed to Herodotus evident nonsense because mountains to the south (and thus nearer the sun) could never be covered with such heavy snows.[12] We now know that Herodotus's informant was at least partly right about the flooding of the Nile and his reasoned disbelief wrong, rather in the same way that his early readers often underestimated his accuracy. This kind of misapplied scepticism provides a vivid reminder of the dangers of relying solely on reason, granted the partial and limited state of man's knowledge – dangers that Golding has been quick to recognise. At any given point in time the scientists and men of reason dismiss what lies beyond their cognisance as fantasy, myth or fairy-tale, as Herodotus's histories tended to be dismissed; but another age may reinstate these rejected theories, having discovered truths behind them.

The central figure of 'The Scorpion God' is referred to

throughout as the Liar, as Herodotus so often was. We gather
that he comes from further north (he refers to the Syrians) and
he has probably been sold into the upper kingdom as a slave,
where he entertains Great House with what seem to his audience absurd and even obscene legends of other lands, of white
men who couple with strange women, of water that is salt, and
of snow – 'the white dust that is water'. Everything he
describes is real enough but these realities are so far beyond
his listeners' imaginations that they reject his stories out of
hand:

> 'Tell me some lies.'
> 'I've told you all I know, Great House.'
> 'All you can think, of, you mean,' said the Head Man.
> 'They wouldn't be lies if you knew them.'

The Head Man is the chief depository of his society's knowledge and experience. As he says, with the hubris of his kind,
'All knowledge is my province. What a man can know, I
know.' Like Francis Bacon, whom he unconsciously anticipates, he is a confirmed rationalist, and his approach to the
unknown delicately parodies the strategems of the realists of
our own times. The Head Man's most pressing problem is the
Nile's continued rise: it has passed the Notch of Sorrow and
the Notch of Excellent Eating, and if it continues to rise it may
reach the Notch of Utter Calamity. His method of investigating the reason for this is to begin by establishing the known
'facts': 'Who kept the sky up? . . . Who made the river rise?'
The answer, obvious to all, is the God, Great House. The
Head Man then argues that since the river continued to rise
after his entombment, 'Something angered him after he
entered the House of Life.' According to this hypothesis, the
likeliest source of his anger was the Liar's refusal to accompany his master to the House of Life, a betrayal that the Head
Man is determined to rectify.

The Head Man justifies his parochialism by logic, but his

limited perspective is exposed when he sets out to reveal the Liar's 'fictions' for what they are:

> 'Do you suppose, my dear, there are real places where people marry across the natural borders of consanguinity? Besides, where would they live, the puppets in these fantastic lies? Suppose for a moment the sky to be so big it stretched out to cover these lands! Well – think of the weight.'
> 'Yes. Madness.'

The rationalist's demystification, used to point up the absurd and comic limitations of his knowledge is a ploy C.S. Lewis often used in his fiction to suggest the existence of the numinous or the unknown. As Lewis was, Golding is irritated by the bland assumption that the rationalists know it all, and that whatever cannot be disposed of as obviously impossible, can instead be attributed to the need to fantasise, and thus be dismissed with a 'Freudian' interpretation. The Head Man goes on to provide a psychoanalytical explanation of the Liar's compulsion to lie. According to this view, his stories of forbidden and impossible things are simply the fantasies that everyone indulges, in 'a desperate attempt to get rid of his own corrupt desires, to act them out in imagination, because – by the laws of nature – they cannot be externalised'. The Head Man, intelligent, wise, kindly and totally wrong-headed is a version of Nick Shales in *Free Fall* or, more distantly and with more caricature, of Golding's own father. His last words as he dies of the Scorpion's sting are characteristically unvindictive, explanatory, calmly analytical. He announces that the Liar has a death wish.

This is the last of a whole series of comic reversals that Golding has built into 'The Scorpion God' as an extension of Herodotus's comment on the Egyptians' inversion of private and public spheres, of which the absurd rationalism of the High Priest is just one more example. The Liar has a death

wish because he prefers life to death and is terrified of the
eternal life of the embalmed corpse in its three coffins which
the Head Man offers him in exchange for 'the vexations, the
insecurities, the trials of a moving now.' In referring to the
Liar's life wish as a death wish, the Head Man implies its
abnormality, its perversity, judged in terms of his own society.
Apart from reversing the phrase's meaning, he uses this piece
of psychoanalytical jargon very much as it might be used
today, to reinforce the dominant values of society. The Head
Man is entrapped within the comically limited horizons of his
society and his whole conception of life is circumscribed by the
usage of the upper kingdom. His ingenious explanations of the
Liar's revelations reveal him to be at once a man of his own
time and place, and yet a recognisably modern figure, too. But
then Golding is sceptical as to how far we have really adv-
anced in the last five thousand years: 'we are not for all our
knowledge in a much different position from the Egyptian one:
our medicine is better, our art probably not so good . . . And
we have a blinding pride that was foreign to them.'[13]

The microcosm of the upper kingdom, narrow both geographically and intellectually, with its rigid code of behaviour,
is not, in the final analysis, so unrecognisably different from
that of Stilbourne, though the relationship is largely one of
reversal: whereas in *The Pyramid* Evie's incest with her father
was the unmentionable, the unthinkable thing, in 'The Scorpion God' Pretty Flower's incest with her father and brother is
considered natural and desirable and it is only copulation
with strangers that seems dirty, a matter for suppressed
sniggering. In the upper kingdom, sex and violence, so carefully concealed or disguised in Stilbourne, are the norm, and
the ten-year-old prince who, like Evelyn de Tracy, wants to be
a girl, is an evident misfit because he does not want to hunt
or 'bounce up and down' on his sister. His sight is failing, and
he knows that he cannot hold the godpose, make the river rise
or keep the sky up. Momentarily the Liar's words enlarge his
world for him, as those of Evelyn de Tracy had done for

Oliver: 'He tells me lies that take away the weight of the sky.'
Oliver had complained that Stilbourne regarded the sky as a
roof. The Egyptians may literally have thought of it as such.
But if the upper kingdom has achieved a stasis comparable to
that of Stilbourne, it is nevertheless a much more precarious
society, whose failure to renew itself is far more perilous. As
the old God fails, leaving an effeminate under-age son and a
daughter, the river rises steadily and the only other figure of
authority, the Head Man, is slain. Without the ruthless, self-
interested and widely experienced stranger to drag them forcibly into a new era, through selfish energy and a more con-
structive rationality that finds a practical solution to the
unpredictable spates of the Nile, the kingdom would have
crumbled and fallen prey to another of the 'dozen petty chieftains that line this river'. Yet though the upper kingdom is
more obviously vulnerable than Stilbourne, its philosophy is
turned not away from, but towards the fundamenatal mysteries of existence: as the blind man explains to the prince at the
outset, 'we live by them.'

'The Scorpion God', Golding has explained in interview,
was written to go with 'Envoy Extraordinary', and there are
some obvious parallels: both depict established and complex
cultures interrupted by crises. In the Egyptian tale this impels
the state in a more positive direction, but in the Roman story
it is suppressed and absorbed. Both are concerned with the
powers and limits of reason and knowledge, while treating
them rather differently. 'Clonk Clonk' was written to 'keep the
other two . . . apart'[14] and it does so by focusing on other
problems; here it is the individual rather than society that is at
risk, and quite exceptionally in Golding's work, the outcome is
a happy one and the dangers retreat. One reason for the
story's unusual optimism may be that it is set quite early in
the morning of the world, in the cradle of society, among men
like children, still unfallen. In some respects a companion
piece to *The Inheritors*, it repudiates the earlier novel's pessimism. A hundred thousand years ago, beneath a smoking vol-

cano which produces natural hot springs, lived a little tribe of
men; yet though they made weapons and fermented alcohol
from honey, they do not as a group seem to have felt
threatened, as Tuami and his companions did. They had
sufficient food supplies and few natural enemies. There was a
sense of life's ample rhythms before time began, of a happy
valley not yet in thrall to civilisation and its discontents,
celebrating a joyous infantilism.

The story reworks a favourite theme of Golding's, that of
the social outcast: the warrior with the weak ankle who cannot
keep up and is ejected from his peer group nevertheless
escapes the fate of Simon in *Lord of the Flies*, Pangall in *The
Spire*, Colley in *Rites of Passage*, and the ending finds him
reintegrated into the group, his powers counting for more than
his weaknesses. This essentially comic outcome might in turn
be linked with the dominant role that women play in the story
and its society: though not a matriarchy in any formal sense,
perhaps less than the Neanderthal people had been, women
nevertheless carry out all the essential functions. Their invest-
ment in the peace, well-being, security and continuity of the
group is constantly in evidence, and epitomised in the character of Palm, she-who-names-the-women. Palm's radiating
warmth, her smiles and kisses, offer a radical alternative to the
harsh and competitive patterns of male rule. She is the most
attractive of Golding's women characters; the way instinct,
impulse and feeling press upon her more ordered thoughts of
duty and responsibility is imaginatively conveyed. The sum of
all that is loving, maternal, protective, Golding characteristically followed this portrait with that of the depraved and
psychotic Sophy of *Darkness Visible*.

The society of 'Clonk Clonk' reveals a deep division
between the male and female spheres of influence. Though
women dominate, they do so secretly, performing the adult
functions in this society: capable and responsible, they initiate
sex, make and drink alcohol, provide the staple diet of 'fish,
eggs, roots, honey, leaves and buds', bear and bring up the

children and care for the old. The men have no essential functions to perform and they behave like and are treated as
children: 'I'm pleased to think of them enjoying themselves. I
only hope they haven't forgotten what they went out for', says
Palm. The men go in awe of the women, regarding their power
as magical and mysterious, like the birth process or the wax-
ing and waning of the Sky Woman. Palm can make the
connection between coupling and pregnancy, but her man is
alarmed by the whole subject:

> 'When I have a baby —'
> Instantly the goosepimples were back.
> 'What is that to do with me?'
> 'Oh nothing, nothing, of course! The Sky Woman does
> it all by herself! However, I haven't had a baby since my
> Leopard Man was killed by the sun. Strange, is it not?'

The men's main contribution, as in most primitive societies, is
to go hunting, yet the meat they supply is hardly necessary
since the women already provide eggs and fish. And quite
often, their hunting expeditions do not even produce meat:

> 'Oh changeless Sky Woman! Not *another* leopard!'

Opposed to the feminine concern for young and old, for communal happiness and survival, the masculine ethos is one of
aggression, personal risk and self-aggrandisement, the hero-
ism of the kindergarten that Golding had so amusingly evoked
in his autobiographical fragment 'Billy the Kid'.

The structural contrast between the social conduct of men
and women finds telling expression in a number of details,
such as their use of names: woman are named after trees, fish,
flowers, *are* effectively what they eat. Their names, once given,
remain constant and their name-giver is correspondingly a
person of authority among them. The men's names, however,
seem to undergo a process of continuous alteration, and any

notable event confers a new and appropriate name on its protagonist which seems to wipe out any previous name from memory. When Palm refers to Cherry and Little Fish, presumably now renamed, the hero does not appear to know whom she is talking about. He himself begins the story as Charging Elephant, is demoted to Charging Elephant Fell On His Face In Front Of An Antelope, and then rejected as Chimp and reinstated as Water Paw! Wounded Leopard! This continual name-changing means that not only their personalities but their relationships with one another are in a state of constant flux. The warrior group is volatile, changeable and sufficiently fluid to reabsorb the outcast. This renaming process has a further function, providing a primitive form of poetry. Golding seems here to hint, and not for the first time, that the moral nature of poetry itself may be as equivocal as this exciting, unstable little group.

'Clonk Clonk' opens on a scene of children playing in their allocated space, and as Golding describes them, the enormous perspective of time folds up like a telescope and its resemblance to a school playground suddenly becomes obvious. The boys and girls are imitating the warrior class, the Leopard men:

> The girls were marching along by the boys in step. They raised sticks together in their right hands. They chanted.
>   'Rah! Rah! Rah!'
> One of the boys was red and crying, already.

The usual story. Golding has admitted that his original inspiration for the Leopard men came from seeing an American university football team accompanied by a band, a 'kind of gross maleness marching to their bus – rah, rah, give me a "D".'[15] Against this assertion of group consciousness represented by the communal chanting, two individuals stand out as such, their particular proclivities conferring on them a degree of separateness and consequently some self-awareness:

Charging Elephant or Chimp, as he later becomes, has a weak ankle that is inclined to give way beneath him. He is a musician who plays the flute, a man of quick intuitive perceptions. As he threads his way carefully down the ravine after the others, he senses that the leopard has passed there last, and though the others later drive him off, it is he who first puts them on its trail; when they celebrate the successful kill, they acknowledge this, and regret his absence, having conveniently forgotten its cause: 'Where was Charging Elephant? We found the trail again. We killed his mighty leopard.'

Palm, the other centre of consciousness, is distinguished from the rest of the women partly by her role of authority. Not only does she name the women (since the men name themselves) but she decides whether a baby is fit to survive or whether it is a weakling who would be a burden on the tribe and must therefore be sent down the river. Palm's perceptions lack the poetry of Charging Elephant's, but she is far more intelligent. For one thing, she has passed beyond the anthropomorphism of her society to a perception of things as they really are: 'The Sky Woman is just the Sky Woman. That is all. To think anything else is to be young – is to think like a man –' (a phrase that, in context, is equivalent to 'think like a child'). An exceptional sensitivity to the world around her allows her to take in the mountain with its threatening plume of smoke and to recognise that the mountain's existence, like that of the moon, is entirely independent of the self-centred little group of bipeds that live in its shadow:

> Sometimes, she thought, the mountain looks up at the sky as if we weren't here; and sometimes the mountain stares down – as if we weren't here! . . . 'A mountain is a mountain! Palm, you think like a man!' . . . All the same, we are *menaced*.

When Charging Elephant describes how his weak ankle goes clonk, Palm sees a resemblance between his physical weakness and her inexplicable misgivings: 'And I go clonk inside. But you can't look into a baby's head,' she tells him, implying that her inner 'clonk' is the mental equivalent of his. But though her fears and his ankle intensify their response to the world around them, are they comparable in any other sense? Palm may have bad dreams, yet her intuition that the volcano beneath whose knees they nestle is indeed a threat, is no senseless or irrational nightmare, like the Inheritors' fear of the Neanderthal people; rather it is a just appreciation of nature's powers.

The climax of the story brings the separate consciousness of Palm and Charging Elephant into juxtaposition and relation. After Charging Elephant has been dismissed by the others with playground cries of 'Go away,' 'We don't like you any more,' he reacts very much as Billy Golding had to his nursery-school experience of rejection, with well-sustained howls of misery and self-pity, quickly followed by self-righteously vindictive and vengeful fantasies.[16] Like a small child, he cries for his mother, long since dead, and loneliness and terror drive him back to the camp where the women are celebrating their secret orgy under a full moon. By now they are very drunk, and fall on him in bacchic fury; it seems that they may even tear him limb from limb. The demented, demanding women fill him with a deep instinctive terror – they are all teeth, even within their wet and hungry orifices. Then Palm comes, and Charging Elephant, now drunk with the alcohol they have poured into him, finds terror giving place to comfort, consolation and desire. It is as if she is the lost mother for whom he has searched, and he has come home.

Next morning Palm insists that Charging Elephant forget what he saw of the grown-ups letting down their hair – it was only a dream. He is finally accepted as Palm's husband and as a Leopard Man again. As in a story intended for children, everything ends happily and all changes are for the best. As in a happy dream, the primitive terrors of being a social outcast, of being suffocated and consumed by avid women, melt and give place to warmth, safety and love. Palm's dream of the threat of the volcano's smoke pall will not come true for a hundred thousand years. Yet her anxiety has a darker edge than she can know. 'What threatens us?' she wonders, and while the obvious answer must be the volcano, there is another and more disturbing one in the warriors' 'Rah! Rah! Rah!' with which the story begins and ends. In this society, at least, male aggression is firmly and safely controlled by wise and benevolent mummies and nannies. But the darkest smoke palls are those created by man.

The third story in the volume, 'Envoy Extraordinary', appeared in 1956, the same year as *Pincher Martin,* and though, like its companion pieces, it is full of fine comic touches, its plot is a little far-fetched and its power lies in its fable, in the dark truths of human nature that Golding invokes but has not invented. The question 'What would have happened had certain discoveries been made much earlier than they really were?' provides the starting point, as it had done in a number of earlier stories, such as Kipling's 'The Eye of Allah'. Golding's story is set on an island, some time during the Roman Empire, where the Emperor and his favourite grandson Mamillius are interrupted by the Alexandrian Greek Phanocles, his mysteriously veiled sister, and his trio of inventions – a steamship, a pressure cooker and a missile that makes use of gunpowder. The variousness of these makes them a little unlikely as the brainchildren of one man, but this is, after all, a *jeu d'esprit*. Evidently the pressure cooker contributes to the sum of human happiness, but the weapons of war are altogether more dubious, and also more difficult to control. The steamship runs wild, and, like a wind-up toy, goes round and round the harbour, conveniently mangling the fleet of Posthumus, the impatient heir who is planning a coup to overthrow the Emperor. When he actually lands, he seizes the missile and aims it at the palace, so that the Emperor is only saved by the intervention of Phanocles's silent sister. She removes the brass butterfly which controls its propelling action. When Posthumus activates it, it blows up on the spot, destroying him and blowing a hole in the harbour where it stood. This provides a convenient solution to the insurrection, but carries darker suggestions of the dangers of weapons of war to their users, the mustard gas that blows back into one's own lines, herbicides that contaminate their handlers and the nuclear weapons that no one can safely use.

'Envoy Extraordinary' has many splendidly comic moments. Attempting to stave off the imminent coup, the Emperor insists on reviewing the heavily armed troops, addressing them with stirring speeches at inordinate length beneath the midday sun; one by one they all collapse from the heat. Subsequently Phanocles offers to invent a magnetic needle to guide his uncontrollable steamship by, and shows the Emperor an early form of printing, thus anticipating Bacon's inventory of inventions that had changed his world – gunpowder, the compass and the printing press. This last invention seems particularly appalling, once the wise Emperor has begun to consider its implications:

'Interesting biographies –' . . .
'Diary of a Provincial Governor. I built Hadrian's Wall. My life in society, by a Lady of Quality.'
'Scholarship, then.'
'Fifty interpolated passages in the catalogue of ships. Metrical innovations in the Mimes of Herondas. The Unconscious Symbolism of the first book of Euclid. Prolegomena to the Investigation of Residual Trivia' . . .
'History – in the steps of Thucydides. I was Nero's Grandmother.'

No wonder Caesar packs the ingenious Phanocles off as ambassador to China where, after all, printing and gunpowder made their earliest appearance, even if not for another thousand years or so. As he wisely perceives, such men are dangerous:

'Oh, you natural philosophers! Are there many of you, I wonder! Your single-minded and devoted selfishness, your royal preoccupation with the only thing that can interest you, could go near to wiping life off the earth, as I wipe the bloom from this grape.'

Though Golding's touch in the stories of *The Scorpion God* is consistently light and deft, he never forgets for very long that history is a peculiarly repetitive catalogue of crimes that have been committed, are being committed and, if we are not very careful, may continue to be committed – with catastrophic results for ourselves and the world we inhabit.

4

Darkness Visible
(1979)

Although Golding has consistently refused to talk about *Darkness Visible*,[1] its central position in the canon of his work is immediately apparent, for this is the novel where he has explored unflinchingly those subjects that trouble and fascinate him most – the extremes of behaviour of which men are capable, their propensities for absolute good or evil, their endlessly paradoxical saintliness and sinfulness. And behind these lie the mysteries of the spiritual world that continually surround us but are largely closed to us, invisible, forgotten or ignored for much of most men's lives. It is these mysteries that Golding penetrates, this darkness that he attempts to illuminate, using two characters who live primarily in a spiritual dimension although at opposite poles within it. The first section is concerned with the nature and visions of Matty who, though physically disfigured, is, in his unworldliness, self-dedication and selfless love, some kind of saint. Opposed to Matty is Sophy, young, beautiful and an agent of the powers of evil, whose impulse towards destruction and primal chaos she advances as far as she can. The book's third section brings the two into direct conflict in the familiar everyday world (now 1978) where the majority of averagely sensual men and women muddle on, neither saved nor damned except by their own triviality. The confusion and dislocation of the modern urban wasteland are vividly conveyed: the high street of the

ironically named Greenfield is filled with the incessant noise of
jets and juggernauts, broken up into distinctive racial groups,
disintegrated by the failure of traditional communal life, a
failure epitomised by the conversion of the parish church into
a so-called 'community centre'. The still small voice of the
spirit that alone gives life a meaning beyond itself, informing it
with energy and beauty, can scarcely be heard amid this
babel, so that Matty is forced to communicate instead by
means of touch and silence. When he examines Sim's palm,
Sim

> fell through into an awareness of his own hand that
> stopped time in its revolution. The palm was exquisitely
> beautiful, it was made of light. It was precious and
> preciously inscribed with a sureness and delicacy beyond
> art and grounded somewhere else in absolute health.

This delicate revelation echoes that of William Blake who, like
Matty, communicated with angels and Old Testament prophets. Blake, too, understood what it meant

> To see a World in a Grain of Sand
> And a Heaven in a Wild Flower,
> Hold Infinity in the palm of your hand
> And Eternity in an hour.

In *Darkness Visible* Golding has plunged into spiritual mysteries which at best may only be seen through a glass darkly, at
worst may be looked on at one's peril. Small wonder, then,
that he has been unwilling to discuss them further, has indeed
prefaced his book with Virgil's prayer as he set out to describe
Aeneas's descent into the underworld and the forbidden sights
he there beheld: 'sit mihi fas audita loqui' – may it be allowed
to me to speak what I have heard.

Darkness Visible spans Golding's career not only in terms of
the centrality of its concerns but also in terms of its starting-

point – a firestorm in the docks during the war. A similar scene of sickening destruction and conflagration, at once horrifying and luminously beautiful, had provided the starting point of *Lord of the Flies*, though it was later cut before publication.[2] The book originally began with a description of the atomic explosion out of which the children escaped, an event recapitulated exactly but in miniature by the fire that is destroying the island at the end of the book; in a comparable way, the naval officer's uniform and sub-machine gun are reproduced on a small scale by the children's war-paint and pointed sticks. Perhaps the description in *Darkness Visible* is the more powerful for having waited all those years to find its appropriate context; its hauntingly vivid detail probably springs from a wartime experience that had not been fully exorcised. But if *Darkness Visible* begins in a man-made inferno, it also begins with a miracle, for out of the fire and the bombs exploding along the street walks a small child. The first response of the fire watchers is incredulity, not only because small children do not normally walk out of fires that are 'melting lead and distorting iron', but because children had no reason to be there at all; they had been the first to be evacuated from the area. And the boy, in spite of all the horrible burns he has suffered down one side of his body, is neither running nor apparently afraid, but walking with a 'kind of ritual gait'. During his subsequent hospitalisation, attempts are made to identify him but it is eventually decided that he has 'no background but the fire' and that 'he might have been born from the sheer agony of a burning city.' Having no name, he is first given a number – seven, the mystic number of the Apocalypse or Book of Revelation; then, two Christian names – Matthew Septimus. When read as a biblical reference, this alludes to Matthew, chapter 7, whose opening verse provides what is to be a major theme of the book: judgement, both in the straightforward sense provided by the verses themselves – 'Judge not, that ye be not judged' – but also in the sense of the final judgement, the judgement

day promised in St John's Revelation. From the outset, everything about the child, known as Matty, is uncertain; for
example, his surname is left deliberately vague. He is to be mis-
named Windy, Wandgrave, Windrap, Wildwort, Windwort,
Wildwave, Windgrove, Windrove, Windgraff, Windrave, and
Windrow until finally, in the last few pages, he is called Windrove, the most appropriate version for a character who from the
first seems to have the ability to disappear, to 'become
unnoticeable like an animal'. At times those around him
wonder, as Mr Pedigree does, whether he is 'all connected with
everything else or does he kind of drift through'.

In the first chapter other hints prepare the reader for other
possibilities. One of the firemen is, in his normal profession, a
bookseller, and as he watches the holocaust over which the
firemen have no control, he ponders its significance:

> The bookseller was saying nothing and seemed to be star-
> ing at nothing. There was a memory flickering on the edge of
> his mind and he could not get it further in where it could be
> examined; and he was also remembering the moment when
> the child had appeared, seeming to his weak sight to be
> perhaps not entirely there – to be in a state of, as it were,
> indecision as to whether he was a human shape or merely a
> bit of flickering brightness. Was it the Apocalypse? Nothing
> could be more apocalyptic than a world so ferociously
> consumed. But he could not quite remember.

Why does the child flicker like this? In what sense is he 'real',
and if he is, how can he remain unconsumed by the fire? On the
first page, the firestorm which is consuming the city is
compared to a 'burning bush', a reminder that God himself
spoke to Moses out of the fire of a burning bush, a bush that
burnt but, miraculously, was not consumed. As in Eliot's *Little
Gidding*, the fire of the Blitz may be purifying, purgatorial as
well as simply destructive, like the annihilating 'black lightning' that threatens Pincher Martin.

Whatever was flickering on the edge of the bookseller's mind, however, it was not only Moses's burning bush. And though the Apocalypse includes many allusions to fire, and provides the most important single reference point for the whole novel, it does not include a comparably flickering figure. The German bombers spraying incendiaries over London have a biblical counterpart in the prophecy of Ezekiel (10:2) where avenging angels scatter coals of fire over the doomed city of Jerusalem. The emergence of Matty from the flames is also reminiscent of an incident in chapter 1 of the same prophecy when Ezekiel beholds a mysterious being:

> And I saw as the colour of amber, as the appearance of fire round about within it, from the appearance of his loins even upward, and from the appearance of his loins even downward, I saw as it were the appearance of fire, and it had brightness round about.

Later, in chapter 8, this spirit carries Ezekiel up to heaven. And if Matty walks into the book like a spirit of fire, so he walks out of it, 'waist deep in gold' and taking the dying Mr Pedigree with him, as 'the gold grew fierce and burned' and Matty vanishes 'like a guy in a bonfire'.

But the Bible is by no means Golding's only point of reference in this opening chapter. The description of the holocaust, which so effectively conveys the agony of a dying city, also has a certain magical quality in all the destruction, a strange brightness, almost a beauty, as though one were looking at a city of the underworld containing 'to much shameful, inhuman light . . . so much light that the very stones seemed semi-precious, a version of the infernal city'. The burning streets become Hell, their glowing stones recalling the building of Pandemonium in *Paradise Lost* (I, 688-730) from which the novel's title is derived. They also suggest the classical underworld with its rivers of flame to which Golding's epigraph has already drawn attention: its words occur just before Aeneas, in the company of the Sybil and carrying the sacred golden bough of mistletoe in his hand as a protective talisman, enters the underworld. Significantly, it is the poet Virgil himself, not Aeneas, who prays to the dark gods to allow him to penetrate the depths and make darkness visible, rather as Golding hopes to penetrate the depths of his society and of human nature.

This patchwork of associations is an indication of how the book is to be read. For the first book of *Paradise Lost*, the sixth book of the *Aeneid* and the Apocalypse have something in common: they are all concerned with twilight zones where judgement is awaited but has not yet been meted out, where things are neither this nor that, and where it is difficult to identify at what point darkness ends and light begins. In this respect both *Darkness Visible* and *Rites of Passage* seem to owe something to Arnold Van Gennep's classic work on ethnography, *The Rites of Passage* (1909), which explores the part neutral zones play in the rituals of passing from one human state to another. It could be argued, however, that much of Golding's work has been preoccupied with situations or states of mind where things are in equipoise. Free fall, in the scientific sense of the term (that is, when gravitational forces no longer operate) is a condition which has always interested him – the point when Neanderthal man died out and *homo sapiens* began in *The Inheritors*; the point when the hero is dead but has not yet submitted to judgement in *Pincher Martin*; the point when paganism ended and Christianity began in 'The Scorpion God'; *Free Fall* and *The Pyramid* may also be said to examine the transition from childhood to manhood. *Darkness Visible* offers more, simply because it attempts more – nothing less, in fact, than an exploration of the most crucial no-man's land of all, where the final battle is to be joined between right and wrong, between good and evil, between darkness and light, and between God and Satan.

Darkness Visible is divided into three parts and, like *The*

Pyramid, clearly derives some of its strength from the threefold
division, the Hegelian form of thesis, antithesis and synthesis
being particularly appropriate for the type of work it is. Of the
three parts of the book, the first – 'Matty' – is probably the
most complex and difficult to understand. The construction is
picaresque, the eponymous hero wandering from place to
place, undergoing a variety of adventures whose significance
is not always immediately obvious. At the simplest level it can
be read as a kind of pilgrim's progress, with Matty seen as the
strange waif of the firestorm who, because of his injuries, lives
out an unnatural and unwanted childhood; in maturity, he
receives a call to put the world aside, including sex, and to
become a sort of prophet – a mission which takes him to
Australia and then back to England; finally he becomes a
charismatic figure exerting a strange power over the men who
earlier in his life had ignored or rejected him. Such simplifi-
cation, however, robs the character of the very thing that
Golding in a variety of ways insists upon – his unreality, his
capacity to merge into the background – even to disappear,
his other-worldliness, his sense of being prophet, priest, king,
and suffering servant all at the same time – in a word, his
intense spirituality.

Matty, we are told, is not very bright but is skilled 'pre-
eminently, in Bible-studies'; his habitual mode of thought, his
repeated questioning of his nature and purpose, and many of
his actions are shaped and conditioned by his passionate and
literal faith in the Bible. On one occasion, for instance,
retreating in haste from the temptations of the flesh embodied
in Mr Hanrahan's seven beautiful daughters, he uses the
words of the Bible almost as a talisman or protective spell,
reciting the whole of the Book of Revelation from the first
verse to the final 'Amen'.[3] Matching Matty's knowledge,
Golding himself, with considerable virtuosity, incorporates
elements of the Bible, from Genesis to Revelation, in his novel
so that it seems that sometimes deliberately, sometimes
accidentally, Matty acts out a series of biblical roles, himself

becoming a changing exemplar of biblical typology. The young boy who limps from hospital, one side of his face destroyed by the fire, has some of the characteristics of Cain in the Genesis story, but even in the first episode at Greenfield a metamorphosis takes place as Matty slips from being Cain to Esau, and then takes on some of the characteristics of Moses.

At the Foundlings School at Greenfield he comes under the influence of a fading former classics master, Mr Pedigree, a man whose name suggests that, whatever else, his lineage is significant; a man who, in the larger context, seems to be the ironic counterpart of the Bible's great progenitor, Adam. Mr Pedigree differs from Adam in having no children, and by reason of his sexual inclinations which are the source of his fall, is never likely to. But he indulges, nevertheless, in a fantasy in which 'he pretended to himself that he was always the owner of two boys: one, an example of pure beauty, the other, an earthy little man!' In this fantasy world, Matty seems marked out for the second role. He is simple and uncultivated, 'his hands and feet were too big for his thin arms and legs. His sexuality was in direct proportion to his unattractiveness,' a fact which, because he is a true innocent, is easily and cruelly exploited by his school fellows. It is the other type of child, the Abel figure, that Mr Pedigree lifts on to a pedestal and on whom he bestows all his special favours; he is exemplified by the boy Henderson, 'a child of bland and lyric beauty'. Under the impression that when Mr Pedigree sarcastically calls him 'a treasure' he really means it, Matty thereafter dogs Mr Pedigree with absolute devotion and cannot conceive that the relationship is based on a joke. In his primal innocence, Matty is literal-minded and unresponsive to the nuances of language. If Mr Pedigree asks him to sit in a corner, keep quiet and tell him when his class fellows do not behave, that is what he does, even though it results in his being despised for sneaking. If Mr Pedigree calls Henderson 'ghastly' and seems to be in great agony of soul because Henderson keeps coming to see him, then Henderson must be 'evil'. Uncomprehendingly, Matty responds to Mr Pedigree's pleas for help against Henderson's loving persecution – with disastrous results.

Soon afterwards Henderson is found dead, having fallen from the school roof, and Matty's gymshoe is found beneath his body. The roof is reached by means of the fire escape, the symbolism of which may now be apparent to the reader, but necessarily escapes the Headmaster and an Inspector who comes to investigate. But the gymshoe is a different matter, raising the question of how it came to be beneath the child's body when he fell. Pressed to explain how it got there, Matty mutters something which the school solicitor mishears as 'Eden' so that he asks the child 'What's Eden got to do with a gymshoe?' Only later, after the Headmaster has retired and has the leisure to think about it, does he feel he begins to understand. Matty was heard to say something about the shoe being 'cast' to which the headmaster had reacted with irritation, remarking that 'it had been thrown, not cast, it wasn't a horseshoe.' But the old-fashioned term comes back to him as he goes over 'the dim fringes of the incident' in his mind and remembers the Old Testament quotation: 'Over Edom have I cast out my shoe,' a primitive curse found in two of the Psalms (60:8; 108:9). Now he begins to wonder whether he has 'the key to something even darker than the tragedy of young Henderson', but he reassured himself that 'to *say* is one thing: but to *do* is quite another.'

This is, of course, exactly where he is wrong. What happened to Henderson is clear enough because Golding tells us: 'No one . . . ever knew . . . how Henderson had begged to be let in and been denied and gone reeling on the leads to slip and fall, for now Henderson was dead and could no longer reveal to anyone his furious passion.' In an obvious sense his death is accidental, the result of extreme distress. In another sense, it is not. Matty had thrown his gymshoe and uttered the Biblical curse, and then, as his journal for 26/11/66 reveals, he had watched Mr Pedigree's window – 'the one at the top that opens on to the leads and where I saw Henderson come away after I had followed him and waited'. Matty had willed Henderson's death and because he possessed a spiritual power that at that stage he did not understand or recognise, his curse was fulfilled and the child fell to his death on the very spot where Matty had flung his gymshoe.

On this dark note the second chapter ends. But there is a further undercurrent that links the misheard Eden with Edom and primitive curses. It lies in two of the Bible's early stories, each concerned with two brothers, and in each of which the elder feels himself to have been unjustly treated as compared with the younger. One is Cain who slew Abel because the Lord paid no regard to the offering he had made, whereas Abel's offering was accepted; the other is Esau (whose other name was Edom and from whom the Edomites were reputedly descended), who is cheated out of his birthright by the smooth trickery of his younger brother, Jacob. The subsequent fate of both elder brothers is that they become fugitives and wanderers on the earth, though in neither case does judgement seem to have fallen on them. Esau is an innocent beguiled; and the mark which God put on Cain was not, as is commonly supposed, to indicate his guilt but as a protection to warn those who saw it that if they attacked Cain, God's vengeance on them would be sevenfold.

The notion of judgement in both these Bible stories is thus as obscure and elusive as the question of who was responsible for the death of young Henderson. To complicate matters even further, there is in Matty's relationship with Mr Pedigree a hint of yet a third early biblical wanderer whose restless journeyings had also begun with the killing of a man – Moses in his youth had slain an Egyptian and concealed his body (Exodus 2:12). Many years later, when Moses communicated with God on Mount Sinai, we are told in Exodus (34:29) he 'wist not that the skin on his face shone while he talked with him'. In the same way, whenever Matty talks to Mr Pedigree the good side of his face, which had escaped the original burning, shines like the sun and indeed when he is trying to give Mr Pedigree an alibi after the death of Henderson, Golding records that the 'sun shone . . . positively ennobling the good side of his face.'

The establishment of a biblical context and a spiritual dimension in the early pages of the book is clearly part of Golding's purpose, not just as an ironic counterpoint, but to suggest the stages of growth that go towards the production of a type of goodness (or Godness) which finally breaks down the partitions that divide ordinary men. The 'Sophy' section works as a contrast; it shows the same principle operating in reverse, thus developing a tension between positive and negative spiritual power, between good and evil forces, between God and Satan, and between light and darkness, which will not be resolved until the final section, 'One is One'.

Sophy's development strikingly parallels Matty's in several particular episodes. Just as his spiritual powers which he does not yet understand become apparent in the episode of Henderson's death, so Sophy's spiritual powers are evident in her throwing the stone that kills the dabchick, an act which an ordinary small girl could not perform if she tried. The incident presents itself to her 'as if it were a possibility chosen out of two, both presented, both fore-ordained from the beginning', involving 'a sort of silent *do as I tell you*'. In other words, like the death of Henderson, it is an act of will operating spiritually or, from another point of view, magically. Of these two acts of untried and indeed unrecognised forces, the cursing and consequent death of Henderson is obviously on a very different scale; yet, deeply wrong though it was, it was prompted by misunderstanding and misguided love for Mr Pedigree. Matty atones for it in full, not only in terms of self-inflicted ordeals (including stabbing his palm with a nail), but in finally giving his life to save another boy of about Henderson's age, and returning after his own death to fetch Mr Pedigree whom he had loved with constancy in the face of total rejection. Sophy's act, trivial by comparison, is nevertheless an act of gratuitous destructiveness. The chick meant nothing to her, yet she took its life wantonly. With similar powers, Sophy and Matty are already developing in opposite directions. Interestingly, near the end of the book, Matty's elders say of Sophy 'Many years ago we called her before us but she did not come.'

Meanwhile Matty must figuratively follow the path that leads from Eden to Apocalypse, suffering along the way the fate of the prophets who warn men in a language that none seems capable or desirous of understanding. Having left the Foundlings School under the heaviest of clouds, he has a short spell as a delivery boy and general odd-jobber for Frankley's the ironmongers, an establishment which is poised between two worlds, one ancient and one modern – an 'image in little of the society at large'.[4] On the one hand there is the nineteenth-century building with its ancient system of accounting and its wing-collared elderly assistants, who live in gloom and have achieved something approaching perfect stillness; on the other there is the new girl in her brilliantly lit bower of artificial flowers, plastic screens, trellises, and whimsical garden furniture, intended to bring Frankley's into the twentieth century and solvency. Into this environment Matty fits like a frenetic Quasimodo or thwarted Vulcan, living in the old coachhouse over the smithy and, in his rare moments of spare time, scrambling about the lofts of Frankley's, trying to catch a glimpse through the skylight of the fair Miss Aylen below, whose scent, grey eyes, and shiny curtain of hair are beginning to put all thoughts of Mr Pedigree out of his mind.

But the veil of Miss Aylen's hair divides him from the Holy of Holies as surely as if it were the veil of the Ark of the Covenant. Other people, at later stages of the book, are to be responsive to the fact that life can rarely be comprehended or, indeed, lived as a whole; that partitions are always there; that 'One is one and all alone, and ever more shall be so.' At this point, the barrier for Matty partly lies in his own realistic assessment that any romantic approach to a girl like Miss Aylen from such a misshapen beast would be a farce and a humiliation; but more significantly, it lies in his sense of guilt for Henderson's death, and in his response, made in prayer and white-hot anguish, to a call which comes to him as he is looking into the window of Goodchild's Rare Books. The catalyst for this experience is a fortune teller's ball or scrying glass which, we are later told, was placed there for reasons that remain obscure by Sim Goodchild's rationalist father. Even though the day is cloudy and dull, the ball blazes as though it contained 'nothing but the sun'. It acts on Matty almost as a revelation, like the mystic moment in *Burnt Norton* when the dry concrete pool seems filled out of 'heart of light'. If the scrying glass blazes magically as a 'heart of light', the Rorschach ink blots that throw Sophy into a fit at a party may be seen as an equivalent 'heart of darkness'. The scrying glass affects Matty the more powerfully simply because it does not *say* anything, is not made up of a whole store of frozen speech as books or churches seem to be, but simply *is* – glowing, illuminating, transforming. Kneeling in Greenfield Parish Church, Matty knows that he has received a call, that he must put the desires of the flesh behind him and try to discover himself and his purpose. He leaves for Australia.

The fact that Matty received his prophetic call from a fortune teller's scrying glass rather than through the frozen words of books, or the conventional medium of the Church, suggests that his subsequent mission to discover himself and his purpose may not follow conventionally religious or biblical paths, may indeed take a more mysterious, even a more magical direction. In his adventures in Australia, one of the main lessons Matty has to learn is the danger of his own literal-mindedness; things are not always as they seem. The Sweets, who employ him in Melbourne, are kind enough, but the girls who work in Mr Hanrahan's sweet factory are far from sweet to him. The wilderness where Matty is stranded on his progress north, with its symbolic 'scrubby thorns' and 'low hump of three trees' is not really the outback, but lies close to the suburbs of Darwin. More particularly, the aborigine who subjects him to near emasculation and mock crucifixion turns out not to be a genuine Abo at all, but simply Harry Bummer, who has 'a fat little woman expecting and two nippers', and has never been the same since they made a film about him. Bummer's pretence at rain-making with the 'small polished stones' is strictly for the tourists. The rain-making 'mumbo jumbo', does however, have its serious aspect. It can be no accident that the dust jacket of the novel carries a reproduction of one of Russell Drysdale's paintings, showing a figure that might almost be Matty emerging from the fire, but is actually called 'The Rainmaker'. And after a period in hospital in Darwin, Matty studies with great absorption the practices of the Abos with their pebbles, before conducting his own strange ceremonies on the State House lawn, building first a tower of matchboxes and then adding, after seven days, twigs and a clay pot. Where the ceremonies differ is that Matty's do not promote rain, but warn against a coming conflagration. He then moves to a large patch of wasteland and sets light to it, and a number of his audience are singed in the ensuing fire. He is called before the authorities because of the trouble he has caused. The secretary, who questions him after this episode is a civilised, highly intelligent man. He knows that ignorant people (those who stand idly round the fire and get burnt; the 'ignorant fellahin' whose first-born were destroyed at the time of the Exodus; the doomed charioteers of Pharaoh's army in the Red Sea episode) will never understand 'predictions of calamity' until it is too late and they are on the point of being engulfed. He carefully explains to Matty that it is precisely the informed and the educated, men like himself, who understand 'the content of the message', but they are also the likeliest to escape its effects: 'The whirlwind won't fall on government; . . . neither will the bomb.'

The nature of Matty's calling and his reason for coming to

Australia now begin to become apparent, though how far Matty himself understands them at this stage remains uncertain. As well as watching the rain-making activities of the Abos, Matty closely consults his Bible before building the tower of matchboxes, and it is clear from a comment he later makes in his diary that he derives his inspiration from Ezekiel: 'I had thought that only me and Ezekiel had been given the way of showing things to those people who can see (as with matchboxes, thorns, shards . . . etc.).'

In chapter 4 of the Book of Ezekiel, the prophet is encouraged to foretell in visual form the destruction of Jerusalem:

> take thee a tile, and lay it before thee,
> and pourtray upon it the city, even Jerusalem;
> And lay seige against it, and build a fort
> against it, and cast a mount against it . . . and
> set battering rams against it round about.
> Moreover take thou unto thee an iron pan,
> and set it for a wall of iron between thee
> and the city . . .

At this point, Matty seems to have moved forward through the Old Testament and is now identified with the prophet Ezekiel: like him, he is in exile (in Australia); like him he communicates through signs rather than through speech; he is very concerned to stay away from images of lust and other abominations (Matty's own 'particular difficulty'); and he only finds the power of speech when the Lord has something for him to say. In this case, the words that finally burst, like golf balls, from Matty's twisted lips, are 'I feel!' – a repudiation of the secretary's unfeeling fluency; his language, pernickety and precise, is inadequate to explain what Matty sees.

Yet the secretary's comments, true enough in their own right, tell us what Matty can see but cannot say. His conflagration of piled-up matchboxes topped with a clay pot are a warning against the 'meteorological gamble' taking place in

Australia where Britain had been testing its first atomic bombs. These tests raised alarming questions not only as to their effects in terms of atmospheric pollution, but also concerning the danger of their use in a future conflict amongst the major nations. The Apocalypse that Matty foretells is not just a warning against those particular tests or even just for Australia. England, as the secretary rightly says in advising his return, needs Matty's warnings more than Australia does.

For the remainder of his time there, Matty's prophetic work is in any case effectively over. There is just one more symbolic act to perform before he shakes the Australian dust off his feet. This incident, in which he goes in search of a place, low down, hot and fetid, and where there is water, is difficult to interpret. Matty's subsequent actions – waiting for darkness, stripping, weighting himself down with chains and heavy steel wheels, and wading through muddy water which at one point completely immerses him, while at the same time carrying a lighted lamp high over his head, does nothing to lessen its mystery. As he performs these actions, Matty loses his individuality, becoming 'the driver', 'the man'. As if watching him from a long way off, Golding suggests that it was all 'inscrutable except inside of the man's head where his purpose was.' Certainly there are strong overtones of a descent into an underworld, whether classical or biblical, in Matty's ritual, particularly as he chooses to enact it in a place where 'even at noon the sun could scarcely pierce through to the water.' The chains and wheels and Matty's heaving up of the lamp to the four points of the compass after he has undergone his ordeal also suggest a ritual cleansing – possibly even a form of self-baptism – before going on to the next stage of his mission. Matty notes in his diary that he has committed a 'great and terrible sin' probably to be interpreted as a reference to his responsibility for the death of the child Henderson. The gospel of St Matthew (18:6) warns that 'who shall offend one of these little ones which believe in me, it were better that a millstone were hanged about his neck, and that he were drowned in the depths of the sea.' Possibly Matty's literal mind suggests to him that an appropriate method of atonement would be to hang millstones (or their nearest equivalent, wheels) around his waist and to immerse himself in that which most closely resembles the depths of the sea. Alternatively, like Dante or Aeneas before him, he may be symbolically crossing from one world into another, and his elaborate ritual might thus be interpreted as some kind of rite of passage, anthropologically speaking.

In the years following his return from Australia, Matty, convinced that he is 'at the centre of an important thing', commits himself to a life of self-dedication, foregoing food and drink, following the precise practices laid down in the Old Testament (in making heave offerings, wave offerings etc.) and preparing for the final judgement which he is sure will come 'in the twinkling of an eye' when the last trumpet sounds. Reading the Book of Revelation one day after his return to England, he becomes convinced that the sixth day of the sixth month of 1966 must be the precise day of judgement forecast in the Apocalypse. The 'awful number' 666 in Revelation is the mark of the beast associated with Rome, and particularly of the Emperor Nero in whose reign the persecution of the early Church was so severe. Matty sees it as his duty to paint the dread number in blood, wear it on his forehead (in fact in his hat band) and to carry it as a warning through the Cornish streets. But nothing happens. At the end of the fateful anticlimactic day, he suffers greatly at the thought of being the only one to feel 'the dreadful sorrow of not being in heaven with judgement all done'. Once again he asks himself 'What am I for . . . If to give signs why does no judgement follow?'

After his return to England, Matty begins to be visited by spirits – one robed in blue and the other in red, both wearing what he naively refers to as 'expensive hats'. Instead of offering him consolation, they warn him that 'Great things are afoot' and tell him that he must throw away his Bible, a direction that makes Matty wonder temporarily whether they are Satan in disguise. It is a kind of obedience test. The discarding of the Bible does indeed seem to be a symbolic putting aside of the Old Testament, the Book of the Law and the Prophets, as a preparation for the New. Matty now seems to take on some of the characteristics of John the Baptist. His spiritual face is scarred by his sin, but he is 'the best material that càn be obtained in the circumstances'. The fact that he seems to be, at this stage, a combination both of the voice in the wilderness, and also a type of the Christ John preceded and heralded, reflects yet again the way in which Matty's biblical roles tend to slide into one another and overlap.

Matty's discarding of his Bible emphasises the change of direction the book is now taking. The final section carries the title 'One is One' a phrase taken from 'Green Grow the Rushes O', or the 'Dilly Song' – an old medieval mnemonic to aid children in remembering some of the basic truths of the Church. In this song the two 'Lily white boys' are the Old and New Testaments in the persons of John the Baptist and Christ. And the change from the Old to the New, beside being hinted at in Matty's discarding the Bible of the Law-givers and the Prophets, is also suggested by the attendant spirits who tell him 'Judgement is not the simple thing you think.' Their warning once again reinforces the message of Matthew 7, the point in the Sermon on the Mount where Jesus condemns the hypocrite who wishes to cast out the mote from his brother's eye without first attending to the beam in his own.

Returning to Greenfield, Matty feels compelled to prophesy against the town that has allowed heathen temples and mosques to grow up alongside the Church of the Seventh Day Adventists. 'Thou Jerusalem that slayest the prophets' he begins, echoing the words of Jesus denouncing the Scribes and Pharisees in Matthew 23:27. Matty claps his hand over his mouth, but the messianic theme is reinforced when his spirits tell him that his mission has to do with a child born on the day when Matty had expected the day of judgement, at which

time a black spirit was cast down. Their words may recall
both the fall of Satan and the birth of Adam in *Paradise Lost*,
books 6 and 7, as well as the defeat of the dragon and the birth
of the child who is to be the Messiah in the Book of Revelation. Structurally, this particular passage is crucial as it
establishes a direct link with the 'Sophy' section and anticipates the confrontation between the forces of good and evil in
the final chapters. At this stage, though, Matty cannot see the
way things are going and is quite unconscious of any threat
from the two little girls he sees entering Mr Goodchild's shop.
Quite the reverse, in fact: 'They were so beautiful like angels,'
he writes, 'I could not help wishing that they were who I am
for.' His attendant spirits are a bit severe with him for getting
it so wrong, but like all the best demonic protagonists, the
Stanhope twins can make themselves appear like angels of
light, and project an outward appearance so attractive in both
looks and behaviour as to prove irresistible to the Goodchilds,
to Roland, to Fido and even, momentarily, to distract the
enlightened Matty from his purpose.

Much later, Sophy, the dark-haired twin, appears to Matty
in a dream that seems to be occasioned by 'my bad thoughts
about Miss Stanhope', and causes him to defile himself. Soon
afterwards Matty becomes the sole witness of Sophy's pretended discovery of her engagement ring, an event which he
interprets as a sign or warning. But he does not pursue its
obvious significance – that Sophy is a liar and must have had
some further purpose in pretending to lose the ring. Rather he
sees it as a symbolic action, translating it to mean 'she does
not care if her jewel is lost', a statement true at another level.
Sophy's 'jewel' could stand for her virginity which she deliberately set out to 'get rid of', but it may also signify her soul. In
Macbeth, a play whose concern with the powers of darkness
makes it particularly relevant, Macbeth speaks of the loss of
his soul in terms of 'mine eternal jewel/Given to the common
enemy of man'. Sophy embodies the temptations of the flesh
which Matty has learnt to see as a Satanic device to divert him

from his mission. Matty's dream explicitly identifies her with the Whore of Babylon in the Apocalypse, a figure generally assumed to represent Rome (this connection is reinforced in the novel by the characterisation of Sophy's father, who has an eagle-like head and sits in his columned room with the remote air of an effete and decadent Roman patrician). St John's purpose in introducing the Whore was to suggest that, after the dragon had been defeated by the archangel Michael, Satan had turned his attention to earth, encouraging the Roman Empire to seduce the early Church from virtue. In a comparable way Milton's purpose in *Paradise Lost* was to show how Satan, defeated in the wars in Heaven, destroyed God's newest creation, Adam and Eve, by undermining their primal innocence. Golding's purpose is more obscure. But Matty's identification of Sophy with the Whore of Babylon alerts us to the fact that she is a figure of unequivocal evil. Her progression from childhood to maturity is as clearly charted as Matty's and her understanding of the process of darkness is as deep and long maturing as Matty's understanding of fire and light.

Sophy's advance towards evil is closely connected with her pursuit of 'weirdness', a concept that even confuses Sophy herself since she recognises that it has several possibilities and is a word that can be used in several ways. The first time Sophy has a 'passionate desire in the darkness to be weird', even though the impulse comes from the unexplored dark tunnel leading to the back of her head, it finds expression in what are on the surface little more than schoolgirl pranks – breaking bad eggs in the drawer of her father's bedside table as a childish protest against his proposed remarriage to Winnie; trying to give Winnie nightmares by 'aiming the dark part of her head' at her when sleeping; later she envisages the unfortunate Winnie, magically incarcerated, Hansel and Gretel style, within her own transistor, to be switched on and off at Sophy's will. Childishly she links such actions with bad smells – 'so eek, so stinky-poo, so oof and pah'.

At this stage, Sophy's weirdness might still be seen as the natural fantasising of a disturbed childhood. But the hints of witchcraft and diabolic possession are there right from the start, and as she grows up, Sophy, like Matty, learns to understand that the pursuit of purity and simplicity, whether it be for good or evil, makes enormous demands. Merely breaking the rules is not enough. Sophy realises that one must 'hunger and thirst after weirdness' with that dedication with which Jesus urged men to hunger and thirst after right-eousness (Matthew 5:6). The inversion of the biblical injunc-tion marks a turning-point in Sophy's pursuit of weirdness, as decisive in its own way as the call which Matty receives when he contemplates the scrying glass. Sophy recognises that 'unless she did what had never been done, saw something that she never ought to see, she would be lost for ever and turn into a young girl.'

In one sense Sophy is using 'weirdness' as a synonym for evil, for no child of the 1960s would knowingly dedicate herself to such an archaic concept as 'evil'. But the word has been carefully chosen for a whole series of associations whose importance emerges gradually. Sophy herself feels 'weird' in the sense of strange when she is caught up in enacting an evil that seems to reach her from outside herself – just as Matty feels the hair rising on his head and goes cold all over in the presence of his spirits. Sophy is also the 'weird' sister, and thus linked with the witches of *Macbeth* whose prophecies of the future teach Macbeth to make them happen by evil means. And this sense of somehow inexplicably knowing the future, knowing what is going to happen next, is another important element in her weirdness, what the child Sophy experiences as 'the "of course" way things sometimes behaved'. She feels that 'as soon as the future was compre-hended it was inescapable.' The Old English meaning of 'weird' was 'fate'. Sensing the future in some way, even being able to shape it to some extent, is, both for Sophy and Matty, bound up with their spiritual powers. It can be no accident that it is the scrying glass, conventionally used for foretelling the future, that becomes the medium for Matty's vision, the call that sends him to Australia.

It is through the dark tunnel at the back of her own head that Sophy knows herself to be different, and recognises, without having words for it, the powers of evil waiting to be exploited – the 'stinky-poo bit, the breaking of rules, the using of people, the well-deep wish, the piercingness, the – the what? The other end of the tunnel, where surely it joined on.' By using people, by denying her common humanity, Sophy can explore the nature of that dark tunnel. And so she embarks on a process of breaking through the partitions into darkness in a way alarmingly reminiscent of Lady Macbeth:

> Come, you spirits
> That tend on mortal thoughts, unsex me here,
> And fill me from the crown to the toe topful
> Of direst cruelty!

In Sophy's case the unsexing is achieved by an act of will. She gives her body as a useless, unnecessary and unregarded thing to anyone who wants it. And in the same way that Lady Macbeth, by stopping up the 'access and passage of remorse', allies herself with the powers of darkness and becomes identified with the Weird Sisters, so Sophy's weirdness now becomes more obviously associated with the traditional picture of witches and witchcraft – an identification accidentally suggested to her after Gerry's libidinous love-making, but denied by Sophy with revealing force:

> 'One day, Gerry, you'll be the filthiest old man.'
> 'Filthy old woman yourself.'
> The grey light washed through Sophy like a tide.
> 'No. Not me.'
> 'Why not you?'
> 'Don't ask me. You wouldn't understand anyway.'

What Sophy might have become had she not made her deliberate commitment to weirdness is clear. She would have developed like Toni. The duality residing in each individual, the uneasy fusion of the spirit which aspires and the flesh which drags down, has always interested Golding. For him human nature is nearly always dual, and Golding usually explores its dichotomies in a characteristic and easily recognisable way, often indicated by the two names which his central characters have or are given (e.g. Christopher/Pincher in *Pincher Martin;* Sammy/Samuel in *Free Fall*). In *Darkness Visible* the nurse who lovingly brings Matty through his worst period of recovery as a child is surprised because Matty thinks of her as two people – she seems to 'bring someone with her'. Matty himself has a good side and a bad side to his face; and there are two Sophys, one who presents a fair face to the world, and the other who sits at the mouth of a black tunnel inside her own head. But now Golding introduces a refinement – twins; girls who, in the eyes of the world, are 'everything to each other', are both beautiful, both of 'phenomenal intelligence' and can both make adults go 'soppy' over them and thus use them for their own purposes. Underneath, however, they are 'as different as day and night'. Toni is the cold one, the intellectual who thinks and is 'out of the whole business of feeling', while passionate Sophy 'broods', cherishing the memory of a rare moment of intimacy with her father.

The main difference between the two sisters is that Toni always lives outside herself (sometimes she seems just to drift away), and Sophy inside. Toni's eyes can see through the back of her head quite easily, as Mr Pedigree finds to his cost when he is stealing books in Goodchild's. But that is because in the back of Toni's head there is nothing. Wild, independent, eccentric, though she can be, she is as transparent as her lint-white hair, and as hollow inside – an easy prey for empty causes like freedom fighting, since she is unable to recognise that such concepts of freedom are a snare and delusion – as much a delusion indeed as believing that by putting on a black wig, she can give depth and substance where no substance exists.

If freedom means anything to Sophy, it is something which involves putting aside all silly posturing and pretending and simply being, simply taking the brake off and allowing the spring to uncoil, because that, in her view, is to be in sympathy with the process of untangling and running down which is the universal law. In its cosmic form she sees this in terms of physical unwinding, or entropy: 'The long, long convulsions, the unknotting, the throbbing and disentangling of space and time, on, on, on into nothingness . . . the hiss and crackle and roar, the inchoate unorchestra of the lightless spaces.' Like Matty, Sophy sees this process as full of significance, a significance which extends even to the pattern of numbers formed by dates. Just as Matty thought 6.6.66 must be the day of judgement, so Sophy sees the date 7.7.77 as no coincidence, but rather part of a larger progress towards unbeing: 'What it wants, the dark, let the weight fall, take the brake off –'. Where Matty senses divine energy, feels himself 'at the centre of things', with time winding itself up to the promised and longed-for fulfilment, Sophy feels exactly the opposite, feels she must collude with collapse and disintegration. And she pictures the end as annhilating waves, 'arching, spreading, running down, down, down –', monstrous versions of the tidal wave that frightened her and Toni when Winnie took them to the seaside. If Matty's element is fire, Sophy's is water. She lives by the river and many of the most important incidents of her life are linked with it.

In human terms the unwinding and running down is reflected in Adam's fall and the apparent triumph of the powers of darkness. And the only way to achieve the final simplicity, to ensure that triumph becomes final victory, is, Sophy recognises, through outrage. It has an inevitability about it, an 'of courseness', a 'weirdness' which, right from earliest childhood when her one-in-a-million throw killed the dabchick, Sophy has learned to recognise as conditioning her destiny. Gerry and his friends might see the kidnapping of the wealthy child as an adventure, an exciting crime suited to mercenary spirits. Toni and her friends might attempt the same thing for political ends. To Sophy, both are profitless, not effectively different from their childhood sport of stealing sweets from the Pakistani shops. Her mind finally comes to dwell on the only thing that really matters, the equivalent of Lady Macbeth's plucking her nipple from the boneless gums of the child that milks her and dashing its brains out; to achieve the final simplicity through outrage. Sophy's sadism is already evident from the episode where she has her first orgasm, brought on not by love-making but by stabbing her boyfriend Roland in the shoulder. At the climax of the story, she fantasises that she has the kidnapped child at her mercy, that she is sliding the knife into his body, that she can feel the sacrificial blood flow and watch the 'black sun' rising in the sky. This final identification of Sophy with Satan, bringing sin and death into the world as a second challenge to God's authority, prepares the way for the last act of Golding's Apocalypse – the saving of the child and the triumph of the forces of good.

The third section of the novel opens in another twilight zone which again throws up echoes of Aeneas's wanderings among the spirits of the underworld who are in limbo and still awaiting final judgement. Sim Goodchild and Edwin Bell are two elderly men, one a bookseller (perhaps the same as that of the opening chapter), the other a schoolmaster. Both are poised between a past that is dead and a future waiting to be born. They represent contrasting types of unknowing and unawareness. Repelled by the noise and confusion of the real world outside, with its jets and juggernauts, ill at ease with the new customs, the new social and cultural groupings of 'the Pakis and Blacks, the Chinese, the Whites, the punks and layabouts' whom they see thronging around them, each in his own way is waiting for a sign. Like Simeon in the gospel of St Luke (2:25) they await 'the consolation of Israel'; unlike him they are not just or devout and will not understand salvation when they see it.

Sim Goodchild, the bookseller, is not, at the conscious level, as aware of this as Edwin. Despite his attempts to think about

'First Things', his waking thoughts are more concerned with fighting fat, inflation, the problems of an old family business going to the dogs, the apathy of a non-book reading public, and his own shortcomings as a man – particularly his 'furtive passion', his interest in the attractions of very young girls. He is cultured in the way of the world, living his life out amongst books, and has a strong literary turn of mind, though an entirely conventional one. All his responses, even at the deepest level, are conditioned by his reading. If Edwin mentions the man in black (Matty, in fact), his mind automatically responds with Wilkie Collins's *Woman in White*. The mere mention of the word 'transcendentalism' touches off the appropriate literary response – 'the great wheel . . . the Hindu universe . . . skandhas and avatars, recession of the galaxies, appearance and illusion'. And just as easily, his illicit feelings for the Stanhope twins are insulated by invoking Wordsworth. In his heart he is conscious that there *is* something else, but 'it is a kind of belief which touches nothing in me. It is a kind of second-class believing. My beliefs are me; many and trivial.' The brute fact of being, the brute fact of believing really comes down to his contemplation of himself alone, locked in the Cartesian tower of his own self-consciousness and other people's words. A rationalist by conviction and president of the local philosophical society, his greatest moment was to act as chairman for a lecture by Bertrand Russell on 'Freedom and Responsibility'; but he is conscious that freedom for him is still only a word, part of a faded poster on the wall.

Edwin Bell, the schoolmaster from the Foundlings, 'cultivated, cultural and spiritually *sincere*', is at the other end of the spectrum from Sim Goodchild. Edwin's line is not mind but spirit (or so he thinks), and he bubbles over in pursuit of the esoteric and the mystical, with the enthusiasm of a schoolboy chasing butterflies. Pursuing the perfect form of all-knowing, when speech will be unnecessary and only the pure language of the spirit will remain, he rarely stops talking long enough to consider the point his quest has reached, clearly, in

Greenfield at least, there is as little need for Edwin's gush of words as for Sim's books.

Into Edwin's sad, distracted world comes Matty – the gardener's odd job man at the rich boys' school to most people, but to Edwin the long-expected one, the nameless Man in Black who has broken through the language barrier and communicates his mystic otherness by extra-sensory means – 'ecce homo', the last hope of an old man desperate for salvation. Unwilling to accept Edwin's frothy protestations wholeheartedly, Sim Goodchild nevertheless allows himself to be led to the park to see Matty, and the subsequent encounter has overtones of the calling of the disciples, with Matty leading the way across the park, a rapturous Edwin and a still sceptical but nevertheless 'interested' Sim trailing in his wake. Largely as a result of Edwin's importunity and Matty's silent acquiescence, the three men form themselves into a small group and Edwin decides that the silence which is so obviously part of Matty's make-up is to be the cornerstone of the group's search for truth. As water was holy to the early Church, so silence is now – 'random silence, lucky silence, or destined'. Such random silence is to be found in the Stanhopes' garden, a 'private place farther down into the earth' where, fortuitously, even the noise of the jets roaring overhead seems muffled. To Edwin it is the obvious place to bring the expected one.

Paradoxically this haven of apparent spiritual peace is also the place where Sophy lives. The 'pool of quiet' that even the rationalist in Sim Goodchild responds to and, in his 'generation-long folly', sees as symbolising the 'innocence' of the little girls who lived there, is in reality another version of the underworld. Sim Goodchild even compares descending into the garden to going under the sea. It is small wonder that Mr Pedigree, who comes reluctantly with Matty to the first meeting and seems considerably more attuned to the reality of what is going on than the others, believes that he is being brought into some 'kind of trap' and struggles to escape. For Matty too, as his journal records, it is a place of evil spirits, 'green and purple and black', which he tries to hold off. The failure of Edwin and Sim to perceive them is a measure of their spiritual blindness or deadness. At another level, of course, Sophy's dwelling place is the home of a 'known' terrorist, part of a genuine underworld of crime and one on which the police have their eye. As Matty and the two old men sit holding hands and sharing what to Edwin seems a magical experience, the hard camera eye above their heads is impartially recording, recording – and trial and judgement are just around the corner.

The scene in the upper room may have something of the mood of the Last Supper about it, for this is the last time that Sim and Edwin will ever again be directly in contact with the mysterious figure who so captivates them and yet whom they are so incabable of understanding. The next time they are to see Matty is in the film of their upper room séance when it is shown as part of the court proceedings following the attempted kidnap. 'It wasn't like that' says Sim Goodchild, trying, like Peter when he denied Christ, to dissociate himself from the accusations and laughter of the gathering crowd, as he watches himself on the television in a shop window, back in the upper room and ridiculously trying to scratch his nose on the table. At the trial and judgement that follow, Sim realises that 'the real public condemnation was not to be good or bad; either of those had a kind of dignity about them; but to be a fool and to be seen to have been one –'. Edwin continues to insist on their innocence, but Sim, in some ways more perceptive, replies 'We're not innocent. We're worse than guilty. We're funny.' Their final confrontation with Mr Pedigree in Sim's shop reverts to Matthew 7:1, 'Judge not, that ye be not judged.' For too long Edwin and Sim have been recognising the mote in the eyes of other people without heeding the beam in their own. Sim Goodchild has been quick to condemn Mr Pedigree for coming into his shop to steal books 'as bait' for children, refusing to recognise that his placing of the children's books in the window to attract the Stanhope girls had exactly the same motive, and was the more culpable in that it was cloaked in pious platitudes about the children's cleanness, sweetness and innocence. He is not the 'sentimental old thing' he pretends but is driven on by 'the unruly member', as his fantasies about the twins reveal. And Edwin might say sanctimoniously about Mr Pedigree 'There but for the grace of God' without seeing any connection with his own sexually ambivalent marriage, that of an effeminate man married to a masculine woman. 'How do I know that I am not speaking to a very clever pair of terrorists?' says Mr Pedigree after the trial. 'The judge said you were innocent, but we, the great British Public, we – how odd to find myself one of them! – we know, don't we?' Such a verdict is no less than they deserve. Both old men have been close enough to feel the warmth of Matty's presence and yet their eyes are not opened. Their fate is not merely to be laughed at, but to remain in the limbo of their own choosing, neither good nor bad. Sim Goodchild at least has some consciousness of the futility of it all, of a paradise that has been forfeited. Cynically convinced of the impossibility of breaking through the circumscribed bounds of life into something finer, convinced that one is one and all alone and ever more shall be so, he yet recollects that when Matty looked into his palm in the upper room, it was 'exquisitely beautiful' and 'made of light'. And the last reference to him sees him pondering on the significance of the whole episode, and 'staring intently into his own palm'.

A purer form of judgement has yet to be achieved – not one concerned solely with moral issues, but one which springs naturally from the spiritual conflict between good and evil. Throughout the book, good has become more and more concentrated in Matty, and evil in Sophy. Now, in a section drawing heavily on the Apocalypse of St John, battle is joined. By this time, Matty recognises that Sophy is to be identified with the Whore of Babylon – provocative, tempting, and very much to be feared. Supporting him in his resistance to her are not only his attendant spirits, increasingly identified with the elders sitting round the heavenly throne, but also other beneficent supernatural forces associated with the magical number seven (Edwin links Matty with 'sevenness'), in turn connected with the healing, generative powers of music and dance. Matty is filled with transports of joy as he listens to Beethoven's Seventh Symphony being played to the children in their music appreciation lesson.

In a final transcendent vision, Matty is shown that he has to bec ome a burnt offering – a necessary sacrifice to be paid so that the forces of evil can be defeated and the child saved who will be the new Messiah and 'bring the spiritual language into the world'. Matty's spiritual face, of which his maimed and two-sided face was a reflection, will be healed, and he too will become an elder. A wonderful being appears 'all in white with the circle of the sun round his head'. He is the angel of the first chapter of Revelation (I:16), out of whose mouth 'went a sharp two-edged sword: and his countenance was as the sun shineth in his strength.' This is the spirit who guards the child, and whose servant Matty has now become. With the elders, he eats with Matty, participating in a form of communion, but when Matty raises his eyes to the angel's face, he is overcome, just as St John had been, and, in John's words, 'when I saw him, I fell at his feet as dead.'

The book now comes full circle. Born out of the fire of a doomed city, Matty endures his personal Calvary as, with his last act, he rushes from the burning school ablaze from head to toe to rescue the child the terrorists are seeking to abduct. Fire imagery increasingly dominates the closing section, warning of the judgement to come and the purgatorial flames through which all must go to achieve salvation. Sophy, on the other hand, is gripped by an uncontrollable rage in which she bitterly recognises that not only has she been thwarted of her prey, but also deserted by her lover for her sister Antonia. But she soon resumes her appearance of calm, smooth-talking her way out of trouble with little apparent effort. The powers of darkness after all can only be controlled for a season and it is entirely appropriate that Sophy should pass from the story still looking like an innocent flower, as she callously betrays the lover who has abandoned her and the father who has spurned her.

It is Mr Pedigree – the man who throughout the book has been most criticised and punished by the standards of the world – who finally becomes the focus of the judgement of Heaven. Like Matty, he has consistently been presented as having a basic innocence of spirit: 'Except for his compulsion' we are told, '– which in many countries would not have got him into trouble – he was without vice.' Indeed Mr Pedigree's worship of beautiful boys might be seen as the beginning of learning to love goodness, though he never actually ascends the ladder of Platonic love. If he is no worse than Edwin or Sim, he has suffered more, having been sent to prison several times and being set upon by indignant housewives. Matty applies to him the biblical phrase 'despised and rejected', and Mr Pedigree differs from the other characters in the book in being more honest, and having paid for his sins – he is more fully human, as he insists in his own defence: 'There've been such people in this neighbourhood, such monsters, that girl and her men, Stanhope, Goodchild, Bell even, and his ghastly wife – I'm not like them, bad but not as bad, I never hurt anybody.' Matty's love for Mr Pedigree may have started as a childish thing but he continues to love the man whom above all others he has wronged. Such love seems to indicate that Matty believes him capable of being saved. Mr Pedigree's 'compulsion' is such that his natural instinct is to resist such a process, and to clutch to himself the brightly coloured ball which is both the means of supporting his weakness and the symbol of his own cherished illusions. Because he senses the unique quality in Matty better than others, he inevitably sees him as a threat – an inimical force, comparable to the 'black lightning' of *Pincher Martin*. Unlike the earlier book, however, the resolution is full of quiet acceptance. All passion spent, Mr Pedigree is in the park, seeming to himself 'to be sitting up to his very eyes in a sea of light'. Sunlight is everywhere, and when Matty comes across to him, he seems to be wading along, waist deep in gold. A 'wonderful light and warmth' seems to surround Matty and as judgement draws near, Matty's face becomes 'no longer two-tone but gold as the fire and stern'. Everywhere there is 'a sense of the peacock eyes of great feathers and the smile round the lips . . . loving and terrible'. Mr Pedigree makes one last effort to resist, 'Why? Why?' he asks, and receives from Matty one word – though not in human speech – *'Freedom'*. The many coloured ball that Mr Pedigree holds against his chest is firmly drawn away and, in agony but also in ecstasy, he crosses the bridge separating one world from another and dies into Heaven – no longer the pathetic old pederast that the park-keeper finds crumpled on the seat, but a soul in bliss. The freedom Matty offers and that Mr Pedigree, however reluctantly, accepts, is starkly contrasted with the illusory freedom for which Toni and her fellow terrorists are fighting; it is closer to the idea expressed in the most famous of John Donne's holy sonnets:

> Take me to you, imprison me, for I
> Except you enthrall me, never shall be free,
> Nor ever chaste, except you ravish me.

It is also the freedom that Sammy Mountjoy, Golding's other flawed and vulnerable human representative in *Free Fall* so long sought for but never found. Viewed thus, *Darkness Visible*, like *The Spire*, is ultimately a hopeful novel, suggesting in its final resolution at least the possibility of escape from a world threatened by atomic bombs, cultural dislocation, ceaseless noise and the tyranny of words.

In another sense the ending of *Darkness Visible* finds Golding as pessimistic as ever about unredeemed man:

> 'We're wrapped in illusions, delusions, confusions' . . .
> 'We think we *know*.'
> 'Know? That's worse than an atom bomb, and always was.'
> In silence then, they looked and listened; then exclaimed together
> 'Journal? Matty's journal? What journal?'

Matty's journal represents the new gospel, the good news that a child has been born that 'shall bring the spiritual language into the world and nation shall speak it unto nation'. The child is guarded by an angel out of whose mouth a sword appears, and on earth by a man who has no certain name, and whose natural mode of communication is in signs, not words. When Matty does speak, it is with the utmost brevity and the words seem to burst out of his misshapen mouth not like swords, but golfballs. 'He's not got a mouth that's intended for speaking' Edwin explains. Matty communicates rather in 'the innocent language of the spirit. The language of paradise.' Matty's elders never 'speak' to him, they 'show', holding out 'beautiful white papers with words or whole books', which he translates into his journal. When Matty asks to be allowed to speak more than he has done, in an echo of the words of Revelation 8:1, 'there was a silence in heaven for a space of half an hour'; then his elders show Matty 'that in the time of the promise which is to come you shall speak words like a sword going out of your mouth,' as the guardian spirit of the child does. Since the only noise coming from Matty at the moment of the child's rescue and his own death is that of burning, it seems that, after all, his journal may yet speak like a sword, but not in the old tainted language of fallen man that the novelist is compelled to use. The optimism of *Darkness Visible* consists in its acknowledgement of the possibility of a new order, of saints walking on earth, of a saviour, a new gospel and a new language. But the promise of a new revelation can scarcely be more than a wild surmise,

> Leaving one still with the intolerable wrestle
> With words and meanings.

Like T.S. Eliot, Golding is left to struggle on under existing conditions, conditions in which the writer cannot escape the guilt of the only words he has to use, and where his fate is not to bear witness himself, but only to imagine the possibility that some day someone else might do so.

5

Rites of Passage
(1979)

There was a man, a parson, who was on board a ship, in a convoy that was going from the east coast of India to the Philippines . . . there was a regiment of soldiers going . . . And one day . . . either he got drunk and went wandering naked among the soldiers and sailors, or else he went wandering among the soldiers and sailors and got drunk and naked, put it whatever way you like. But he came back, he went into his cabin and stayed there and no matter what anybody else said to him he just lay there until he died, in a few days . . . I found that it was necessary for me, for my peace of mind, to invent circumstances in which it was possible for a man to die of shame.

So Golding has explained the genesis of *Rites of Passage* from an incident recorded in Scawen Blunt's diaries, in which the young Duke of Wellington was also involved.[1] The novelist's interest in it is characteristic, another instance of his preoccupation with 'man at an extremity, . . . man isolated, man obsessed'.[2] The capacity to die of a socially induced emotion such as shame must always have been rare; in our own late twentieth-century society it seems particularly alien and difficult to imagine – shame is an undesirable, unreasonable feeling. The victim of such a fate must inevitably appear absurdly, pathetically over-sensitive, someone who has allowed a trivial indignity to be blown up out of all proportion, someone signally lacking in the virtues of honour or common sense. With the artist's instinct for balance, Golding offsets the parson Colley's pained account of his experiences with an alternative version of the voyage, set down by a figure who is Colley's antithesis in most respects. Edmund Talbot, the book's main narrator, is a young man of the world who, in his ordinariness, his average sensuality, to some extent corresponds to the common reader, anticipating and cushioning reactions of disbelief, shock, perhaps even wonder. Talbot combines a prosaic good sense that we flatter ourselves is typically modern, with an eighteenth-century cynicism and an overview of life firmly centred on man and his institutions. Yet the book's complex ironies allow Talbot's journal to expose the limitations of his sympathy and imagination; his various blind spots reveal the shortcomings of this kind of outlook. Ultimately, it is suggested, Colley's extremism, his romantic follies, his agonies and ecstasies provide a fuller and deeper record of the human condition.

Golding would probably find such an account of the book too serious, too 'po-faced'. He has argued that it should be read as an entertainment, insisting that though the comedy is inevitably black – as what comedy today is not? – much of the book is 'just funny'.[3] And certainly there are some memorably comic moments: the hasty coupling of Talbot and Zenobia under the tumbling contents of his library shelf, disastrously interrupted by the off-stage discharge of the blunderbuss; Talbot's noisy convulsions and involuntary groans interpreted as over-zealous prayers; the drunken Brocklebank taking Summers's place and marrow-bones at the Captain's table; the seasoned soldier Oldmeadow fainting at the sight of a corpse, as well as a series of conversational misunderstandings and sharp put-downs. Yet Golding's delight in and admiration of social comedy may incline him to over-estimate the importance of this element in his work: 'If someone would present me with a great social comedy, I think I would go very near to selling myself' he has told John Haffenden.[4] Despite his aspirations towards comedy, his vision is essentially a sober one, of man as a moral being and a desperately flawed one at that. His farcical moments are more inclined to arouse pity for human folly than a joyous or carefree laughter. Social comedy, both here and in *The Pyramid*, seems rather to be accompanied by a darkening vision which *Darkness Visible*, for all its evident horrors, finally evades through its compensating glimpse of a transcendent goodness.

Edmund Talbot's journal, though by no means a document to be taken at face value, offers its reader (ostensibly his godfather) some notion as to how it (and by implication the book as a whole) should be read:

> It is the last page of your journal, my lord, last page of the 'ampersand'! I have just now turned over the pages, ruefully enough. Wit? Acute observations? Entertainment? Why – it has become, perhaps, some kind of sea-story, but a sea-story with never a tempest, no shipwreck, no sinking, no rescue at sea, no sight nor sound of an enemy, no thundering broadsides, heroism, prizes, gallant defences and heroic attacks! Only one gun fired and that a blunderbuss!

Judged in these terms, there can be no doubt as to the book's effectiveness. It *is* witty and full of acute observations – though perhaps not exactly of the type that Edmund Talbot has in mind. It is also wonderfully well and fluently written, with none of the passages of over-writing which sometimes mar the other books. Constraints are created by relating events through a journal and a letter, a technique suggesting an element of eighteenth-century pastiche that in turn generates its own internal controls, while allowing Golding to rise to the type of challenge he relishes. The pastiche lacks the scrupulous attention to detail as it lacks the affectation of, for

example, John Barth's *Sotweed Factor*. Anachronisms occasionally creep in. The words 'loo' (a privy) and 'sky pilot'
(nautical slang for a clergyman) both belong to the late, rather
than the early, nineteenth century. And there seems to be an
allusion to De Quincey's *Confessions of an Opium Eater* in Wheeler's reference to 'a gentleman ashore as has wrote a book on
it', as he tries to ply his young master with paregoric (an
opium-based drug). Golding puts the date of his sea voyage at
round about 1812 or 1813;[5] De Quincey's book was first published in 1821. But as with the trivial anachronisms of 'The
Scorpion God', such touches tend to contribute to, rather than
detract from the rich period flavour. Following the example of
various illustrious predecessors, Golding has always used the
artist's privilege of extracting from reality only what he needs
for his immediate purposes. *Rites of Passage* feels like a genuine
story of its time and that is enough.

As an entertainment, the book might well bear the pedantic
subtitle that Edmund Talbot himself mockingly gives it: *The
Fall and Lamentable End of Robert James Colley together with a Brief
Account of his Thalassian Obsequies*. If it lacks the variety of
incident to be found in 'lively old Fielding and Smollett',
whom Talbot seems to prefer to 'sentimental Goldsmith and
Richardson', it still has a wide cross-section of characters most
of whom, in the picaresque tradition, are two-dimensional
representatives of their type and class: the 'notorious free-
thinker' and 'inveterate foe of every superstition' (Mr Prettiman); the tough-minded governess who has come down in the
world (Miss Granham); the grotesque and bibulous portrait
painter and pander (Mr Brocklebank); the ageing and his-
trionic whore (Zenobia); the down-at-heel no-class parson
(Colley); the lieutenant with the heart of gold (Summers); the
cheerful and amoral jolly jack tar (Billy Rogers). And though,
as Talbot says, it is an untypical sea story in its lack of action
intruding from the outer world, no one could complain of lack
of action from within; the story throws up all sorts of mysteries
as it progresses, most of which are resolved or partly resolved

by the end of the book. Why is it not a happy ship? Why have the officers been specially gathered together for this trip? Why does the Captain hate parsons? Who is the purser, and why does everyone fall silent at the mention of his name? What inside information does Lieutenant Deverel possess concerning the Captain? What is the 'badger bag'? What was the coincidence Deverel laughed at when Talbot told him of his plan for unloading Zenobia on Colley if she became pregnant? What mysterious power does Wheeler have and how does he know so much? How did Wheeler come to fall overboard?

Above all, there is the central mystery of the book – what happened in the fo'castle which resulted in Colley's dying of shame? Who, to echo Brocklebank's brutal words, 'killed cock Colley'? The answers to this, and to many other questions as well, emerge less in fictional than in dramatic terms, and Talbot in telling the story, finds himself turning to the language of the theatre. His journal becomes 'the record of a drama – Colley's drama'. On more than one occasion he attempts to define the nature of the drama he is witnessing. The first time occurs only half-way through the book, after the crossing-the-line ceremonies, but long before Talbot has realised how traumatic these were for Colley: 'The last scene, surely! Nothing more can happen –' he crows, but he could not be more wrong, just as he is wrong about the nature of 'the play. Is is a farce or a tragedy? Does not a tragedy depend on the dignity of the protagonist? . . . A farce, then, for the man appears now a sort of Punchinello.' By the end of the story, when Talbot has read Colley's own account of events, he revises his opinion: now he sees what has happened in terms of a 'tragic trilogy' after which the explanation for Captain Anderson's loathing of parsons provides a kind of 'satyr play' that 'comes limping after'. And as if these references to life imitating art were not enough, the book ends with the further irony that the passengers, once 'the poor man's drama is done', plan to put on a genuine play for the lower classes at the 'forrad end', to while away the time during the remainder

of the long voyage. Zenobia has already displayed her theatrical talents. Meanwhile Colley's tragedy has ended just south
of the equator, leaving us wondering how many more dramas,
whether real or imaginary, might be played out before this
Ship of Fools finally reaches its destination in Australia. Golding has encouraged such speculations, saying in one interview
'just because my ship has got from the coast of England a little
beyond the equator, don't think its voyage is finished. You
could get another couple of volumes about that voyage, if you
wanted.' And, even more promisingly, 'I still find myself
thinking of things I wish I'd made Talbot say – but the voyage
is still young!'[6]

Golding himself has justified the powerful presence of
theatrical metaphors (one of several links with *The Pyramid*,
which shares with *Rites of Passage* themes of snobbery and
self-exposure): 'It had to be theatrical because (Colley) had to
make an exhibition of himself, and therefore the ship had to be
turned into a theatre in which he could do it.'[7] So it is that the
ship provides a natural forum, with its decks simulating the
various stages. The fo'castle has two side doors opening out on
to what becomes the main stage, and the higher class passengers are housed in the galleries of the quarterdeck, the better
to observe the action on the inner stage. The plot, as revealed
by Talbot's diary, also follows a three-act division, or else, as
he sees it, a tragic trilogy. When the events are set out in their
proper time sequence, act one presents the general situation
and all the possibilities of conflict, particularly the rivalry
between Colley and Talbot as representatives of Church and
State, and between both of them and Captain Anderson. In
Colley's case, this is the result of an apparently irrational
antipathy the Captain holds towards men of the cloth. Act two
shows where such conflict leads and anticipates the tragedy to
come. Abandoned both by Talbot and the Captain to the
many hostile influences around him, the unworldly parson
blunders from folly to folly. This act reaches its climax in a
mysterious event offstage, so appalling as to lead to Colley's

death, as an act of self-will. Act three is a long denouement in which everything, or nearly everything that has happened is explained. The Captain's inquiry following Colley's death seems to approach the truth by a series of gradual revelations. It was not the indignity of the 'badger bag' (naval slang for the crossing-the-line ceremonies, or persecutions, presided over by King Neptune) during which Colley was forcibly bathed in ordure, that had led him to bury his head in his pillow, never to raise it again. After all, as he rightly insisted, 'What a man does defiles him, not what is done by others.' It was not that he had got 'drunk as the butcher's boots' when he had gone amongst the crew 'to deliver a rebuke' for the insult to his cloth. It was not for the renewed insult when his clerical dress, which he believed to be so much more authoritative than he was, was torn away. It was not that he had openly urinated in front of the passengers and crew. It was not even that his own latent homosexuality had been revealed to him. It was – so the court finally agrees in the neutral jargon that covers such delicate situations – that some sailor or sailors unknown had 'inflicted a criminal assault on the gentlemen so that he died of it'.

But Talbot knows better, knows, perhaps, more than he realises he knows. He had seen the parson emerge from his encounter with the crew 'in a state of extreme and sunny enjoyment'. He had heard him cry 'Joy! Joy! Joy!' as he returned to his cabin, and had watched him walk 'head up and with a smile as if already in heaven' to the ship's latrine. Whatever had happened in the fo'castle to destroy him, Colley had paradoxically found it joyous. And in a surprise ending to the drama, Talbot, whose general worldliness, as well as his interest in 'tarry language' makes him more alert to what is going on than the less sophisticated Mr Prettiman and Miss Granham, learns from a chance overheard remark and from reading Colley's self-revelatory letter to his sister what had *really* happened on the fateful day. Colley, while scarcely realising that he was doing so, had been living out a secret life

red on a handsome young sailor. He had initially concealed from himself his true interest in Billy Rogers by seeing
him as a 'sad scamp . . . whose boyish heart' had 'not yet been
touched with grace', and who yet might be saved for the Lord.
But as the voyage had progressed, as the passengers' indifference and the Captain's prohibitions had driven him deeper
into himself, he had been increasingly confined to a kingdom
of his own in the waist of the ship. There he had become more
and more preoccupied with Billy Rogers. Perhaps he would
have remained so harmlessly enough had not loneliness and
the fiery liquor with which he was tempted awakened in him
the desires he hardly knew he possessed. Drink plus the memory of his sailor hero provocatively stretched out along the
phallic bowsprit, had been too much for his simple soul. He
had followed his yearning 'to kneel before him', not to praise
or pray but, when the opportunity was offered, to commit
fellatio. And the shame of his public denial of everything he
hoped to be had broken his heart. This was the knowledge
that Talbot and Talbot alone possessed, and to a man who
had always doubted Colley's religious convictions and seen
him as just the other side of the coin from Zenobia – 'the one
in paint pretending devotion, the other with his book *surely
pretending sanctity*' – the knowledge might even have brought
some satisfaction. But Talbot had read Colley's long letter to
his sister, and learned from it that Colley was no simple
hypocrite. The loneliness created by his cloth and his class
had told Colley 'things about himself which he did not know,
things of which he had no conception till he took counsel with
the great solitude – and the whisper had proved irresistibly
fascinating'.

These words refer to Kurtz's encounter with the *Heart of
Darkness* in Conrad's novel of that name. Its events are echoed
more directly when Talbot decides to appropriate Colley's
tormented letter to his sister and substitute for it a series of
kinder lies, very much as Marlow, the narrator of *Heart of
Darkness*, felt obliged to conceal from Kurtz's fiancée what
Kurtz had become in Africa:

I shall write a letter to Miss Colley. It will be lies from beginning to end. I shall describe my growing friendship with her brother. I shall recount all the days of his *low fever* and my grief at his death.

Colley, though obviously very different from the sinister figure of Kurtz, was, as Talbot admits in his final summing-up, in his own way exceptional. Not for him the small steps of vice carrying the Brocklebanks of this world towards the everlasting bonfire:

> What a thing he stumbled over in himself! . . . Just as his iron-shod heels shot him rattling down the steps of the ladders from the quarterdeck and afterdeck to the waist; even so a gill or two of the *fiery ichor* brought him from the heights of complacent austerity to what his sobering mind must have felt as the lowest hell of self-degradation. In the not too ample volume of man's knowledge of Man, let this sentence be inserted. Men can die of shame.

And with this summation we are brought back to Golding's starting-point for the novel, the need to invent circumstances in which it was possible for a man to die of shame. If that was all his purpose, he has triumphantly succeeded.

But such a bare outline of events scarcely indicates the book's most central concerns: other preoccupations recur, the most obvious of these being class, the destructive power of which had been demonstrated intensely and comprehensively in *The Pyramid*. And some account of the unshakable gradations of life on board ship had been given several years earlier, in an essay entitled 'A Touch of Insomnia'. Here Golding described the tedium of crossing the Atlantic in a liner in which[8]

> the class system was axiomatic. You could not invade a plusher bar simply by readiness to pay more. Nor could

you descend to a less comfortable pub if you wanted to pay less. Where you were born, there you stayed. At the beginning – a sort of privileged babyhood – you could glimpse the other worlds. You could pass through doors marked First Class and see the wide bedrooms, the stupendous still lifes of sea food on the side tables of the dining-room . . . after that the doors were locked. We had to be content with our middle station, right aft, where you got any vibration that was going. And I supposed there was some sealed-off hold where the base of our social pyramid rested; where tourists were chained to the kelson under the whips of savage taskmasters, while their flesh was subdued by a diet of weevily biscuits and stale water.

Shipboard life here, as in *Rites of Passage*, is a microcosm of the rigid British class structure that cannot be left behind. In the novel, the passengers are divided into those with cabins (two dozen of which are arranged around the mizzen mast, with its dining saloon aft) and the common people, the 'emigrants', as they are referred to, who are huddled together at the front of the ship and divided from the ladies and gentlemen by a white line across the deck which only the sailors and the imprudent Colley cross. Dining with the Captain is, as always, regarded as a rare and special privilege, but the first lieutenant, Summers, invites the gentry to a glass of wine in the saloon. Talbot comments 'I have found out since, that they have heard such gatherings are customary in packets and company ships and indeed, whenever ladies and gentlemen take a sea voyage.' The protocol of the modern liner is thus only a more complex version of the social rituals of *Rites of Passage*.

Like Oliver in *The Pyramid*, Edmund Talbot is more than usually conscious of the 'infinitesimal gradations' which separate people, and perhaps slightly envious of those whose 'rank and position in society put them beyond the vexation of such trivial social distinctions'; among their number his godfather and patron must be included. 'You have set my foot on the ladder,' writes Talbot with appropriate servility, 'my ambition is boundless' – the clear implication being that the more rungs of the social scale he can climb, the better. At the start of the voyage, having decided that, with the possible exception of Lieutenant Deverel, he is the most well-born and well-educated person aboard, he behaves with an insensitive arrogance that he imagines his social position allows. His cabin is merely a 'sty', unfit for human habitation. He shows off by speaking Greek to a callow midshipman and notes with pleasure how the irascible Captain can be tamed by the mere mention of his godfather, observing 'what a silver-mounted and murdering piece of ordnance a noble name was proving to be among persons of a middle station'. In particular, his contempt is reserved for the parson Colley who 'has stepped out of his station without any merit to support the elevation', a fact observable in his physique, speech, 'habit of subordination', and his inability to hold his liquor. Colley appears to Talbot as living proof of Aristotle's teaching, that men belong by nature to a particular place in the social hierarchy. Colley's face is that of a peasant, therefore 'his schooling should have been the open fields, with stone collecting and bird-scaring, his university the plough.' And he reverts to the same thought at the climax of Colley's tragedy, when the drunken parson sings lewd songs: 'A peasant, born to stone gathering and bird-scaring, might have picked them up under the hedge.' Only the despised rationalists, Miss Granham and Mr Pretti-man, are sceptical of the significance of class distinctions, and the advantages supposedly conferred by birth and breeding.

But Talbot is not all bad. Like Jane Austen's Emma, his snobbery and class consciousness are not so deeply ingrained as to destroy him completely. At times he may play the silly ass, but he has some capacity for growth – an innate good sense, a receptivity to the lessons of experience – which sug-gests that, even without the help of his influential patron, he might well develop into a good assistant Governor of Australia. If, as seems to be suggested, his favourite author is William Cobbett (the most notable contemporary scourge of 'scurvy politicians'), the inference is that a certain pragmatic radicalism tempers his habitual Tory position. And he does learn a little from experience. After he has warned Captain Anderson obliquely that his injustice to Colley has been recorded in his, Talbot's journal, he watches the Captain come down to the lobby with an air of indecision, and congratulates himself on the success of his intervention: 'This was a modified triumph, was it not?' But the next chapter begins 'Wrong again, Talbot! Learn another lesson, my boy! You fell at that fence! Never again must you lose youself in the complacent contemplation of a first success!' Talbot finds a similar necessity to revise his attitude towards the first lieutenant, Summers. Summers had once been a common sailor but had, as he explains in the tarpaulin language Talbot is so keen on acquiring, come 'aft through the hawsehole'. In the first instance Talbot had reacted to his elevation in the way any young buck might have done, with condescending congratulations to Summers on his ability to *imitate* 'the manners and speech of a somewhat higher station'. It is Lieutenant Deverel, 'the most gentlemanlike officer' and 'an ornament to the service' to whom Talbot is initially drawn. To his credit, however, Talbot is persuaded by events aboard that his own 'knowledge of the springs of human action' is 'still in the egg'; that Deverel, far from being an ornament to the service, represents 'the last decline of a noble family' and that it is really Summers, with his passion for fair play and justice, that is 'the person of all this ship who does His Majesty's Service the most credit'. What prompts Talbot's advance in self-awareness and an element of self-reproach is the discovery of Colley's letter to his sister. This reveals that Colley's friendliness towards him, which he had misread as the natural sycophancy of the social climber, arose from a genuine esteem. It also reveals the part Deverel played in victimising Colley in the 'badger bag', and that his action was partly inspired by petty revenge: Colley had interrupted the officer as he fought with Cumbershum over Zenobia's letter.

Nevertheless, it would be reading altogether too much into the novel to suggest that Talbot suffers a sea change which will long outlast the events of the voyage. As with Oliver in *The Pyramid*, enlightenment comes, but it comes too late, and the cost of further self-knowledge is too high to be paid. 'Class,' as Summers perceptively remarks, 'is the British language,' and too firmly rooted in the subjects of that tight little island to be more than temporarily disturbed. Once Colley is at the bottom of the sea with cannon balls at his feet, Talbot, like Richard the Third, is soon 'himself again', ready to put the diplomacy of his class to use in drafting a letter to Colley's sister which will contain 'everything but a shred of truth'. Like Oliver, there is much that he still fails to recognise. Overhearing a conversation between Prettiman and Miss Granham on someone whose opinions are described as 'Gothic', he fails to realise that he himself is the benighted victim of their conversation. And he is totally obtuse about the cause of Wheeler's death: '"At least," said I to Summers with meaning, "no-one can accuse me of having a hand in *this* death, can they?"' Yet it seems distinctly probable that Wheeler was murdered because it was (wrongly) supposed that he leaked information about Colley to Talbot, who had attended the enquiry on his death. The white line that separates the fore passengers from the aft remains as immaculate as when the ship set sail. Colley's rashness in attempting to cross it provides a solemn warning of the dangers of breaking such a strong territorial taboo without recourse to the appropriate rites.

Rites of passage in the widest sense – both anthropological and symbolic – lie at the heart of the novel. Thematically the book is about transition. One early reviewer, John Carey, interpreted this primarily in literary terms: for him, 'The contrast between the two journals, and between the minds they mirror, is the pivot of the novel and . . . of a whole phase

of English intellectual history.'[9] There is much to be said for
this view. The manner and contents of Talbot's journal do
link him firmly with the 'moribund grandeurs of Augustan-
ism' in the same way that 'Colley's blend of poetry, mysticism
and nature study' relate him to emergent Romanticism. Talbot's journal is insistently focused on himself and the little
world of human action around him. He likes to 'expatiate free
o'er all this scene of man', but the wider world of nature leaves
him cold. His account of the voyage gives little impression of
the weather, and his brief essay into description of his sur-
roundings soon collapses under its own self-consciousness:
'the billows sparkled, the white clouds were diversedly mir-
rored in the deep – *et cetera*'. The artificial character of Augus-
tan diction at its weakest is apparent in the use of 'billows' and
'deep'. It is not till we reach Colley's letter that we are made
aware of the power and beauty of nature. Though still ill with
sea-sickness, Colley declares 'how remiss I have been to
repine at my lot! It is an earthly, nay, an oceanic paradise!
The sunlight is warm and like a natural benediction. The sea
is brilliant.' Later descriptions of a thunder storm and then of
a strange white mist that hangs round the ship recall Coleridge's *Ancient Mariner*, as Colley's ordeal of loneliness and
victimisation symbolically links his fate with that of the
Mariner. This poem, one of the greatest and most seminal of
the new age, figures as importantly in *Rites of Passage* as
Macbeth had done in *Darkness Visible*. And as that play's evil
spirits are invoked by Sophy, so the redemptive powers of God
and nature referred to by Coleridge are invoked by Colley. Yet
it is not Colley but the tawdry Zenobia who first refers to the
poem, adding that she has met its author: 'Mr Brocklebank –
pa – had painted his portrait.' Mr Prettiman then determines
to shoot an albatross to prove to all the folly of superstition but
as he parades the deck with his antique blunderbuss in search
of one, he seems rather to prove 'how really irrational a
rationalist philosopher can be!'

In choosing the moment of conflict between the enlightened

eighteenth century and the darkening glass of romanticism, Golding has chosen yet another important moment of historical transition, a moment of change-over such as he had built into his earlier historical novels, *The Inheritors*, *The Spire*, and 'The Scorpion God', as the focus of his myth. *Rites of Passage* certainly includes a number of points of resemblance to his earlier novels, though Golding understandably finds critical emphasis on the continuities rather than the differences between his novels irritating. Creative artists nevertheless tend to write to certain patterns that are as individual as a fingerprint, though very much harder to classify, and this is as true of Golding as of any novelist writing today. Like *Lord of the Flies*, *Pincher Martin* and *The Spire*, *Rites of Passage* uses a fixed and limited location (an island, a barren rock, a cathedral, a ship) as a metaphor for the human condition. As in *The Inheritors*, its viewpoint is changed towards the end when a sequence of events is suddenly seen through different eyes. Like *Pincher Martin*, it is a sea story, but a sea story with a difference. Like *Free Fall* (in the episode dealing with Father Watts Watt) and *The Spire*, it probes the dilemma of the priest whose soul aspires and whose body conspires against him. Like *The Pyramid*, it is almost obsessively concerned with class and the damage it causes. And as in *Darkness Visible*, its inner significance lies in the rites of passage that exist between one state and another and the mysteries that underly the ceremonies of transition.

In comparison with Golding's other novels, *The Spire* seems particularly significant as a predecessor: both novels conform fairly strictly to the unity of place, the action of the one taking place within the claustrophobic confines of a crowded ship, and the other in a cathedral. Both ship and cathedral seem to possess an organic life of their own which closely reflects the sexual dilemmas of their protagonists. Jocelin's lust for Goody Pangall was anticipated in an early description of the cathedral itself as a recumbent male figure, arms outstretched, with the bowels or grosser parts represented by the pit and the stirring of septic sludge from the adjacent graveyard, the penis by the phallic thrust of the spire. Colley's more ambivalent sexual desires in *Rites of Passage* are appropriately expressed by a ship which is redolent of sexual energy, but in a seemingly androgynous form – it possesses traditional female characteristics in the figurehead and sails which, when filled with wind, resemble an old lady lifting her petticoats; yet as well as the sails, there is the more masculine forward-thrusting bowsprit. Male or female, however, there is no doubt what the nether regions of the ship represent. With their 'rotten bilge of gravel and sand' smelling like a graveyard, they fulfil the same role as the pit in *The Spire*, both in suggesting the bowels or grosser instincts, and at the same time generating a sense of mystery, of infernal otherness which is clearly present but never fully understood. This sense is personified by the enigmatic figure of the ship's purser, a peculiar creature with a vast head and small spectacles, who never appears on deck but spends his time poring over a ledger in his kingdom below, as if studying the Book of Judgement. Officers and men alike are apparently afraid of him. The mere mention of his name is enough to promote silence and unease 'as if the man were holy, or indecent' (words that seem more obviously appropriate to Colley than to the mysterious purser). One reason eventually emerges for the silence caused by any mention of him: all the ship's officers owe him money. But it may be that the purser plays an altogether more sinister role than that of accountant, whether literal or spiritual. This is indirectly suggested by Lieutenant Cumbershum who, when talking about the strangeness of the ship and its voyage, remarks that 'the devil is in it.' The purser resides over a kingdom of the underworld which has the smell of corruption about it. But it is also the repository of the ship's wealth, the assets that keep it functioning:

'Tools, adzes and axes, hammers and chisels, saws and sledges, mauls, spikes, trenails and copper sheet, plugs, harness, gyves, wrought iron rails for the governor's new balcony, casks, barrels, tuns, firkins, pipkins, bottles and bins, seeds, samples, fodder, lamp oil, paper, linen.'

'And a thousand other things . . . ten thousand times ten thousand.'

This view of another kingdom, mysterious, inimical, provides another link with *The Spire,* which shares with *Rites of Passage* a preoccupation with the tension between pagan and Christian beliefs. If one asks what *are* the rites of passage which are the subject of the story, it is clear that they fall into two contrasting categories. On the one hand much is made of the fact that, at one time or another during the voyage, all the main occasions requiring Christian rites occur: 'What a world of conflict,' says Talbot, 'of birth, death, procreation, betrothals, marriages for all I know, there is to be found in this extraordinary ship!' And later we find him hoping that the Captain will marry the betrothed Miss Granham and Mr Prettiman 'so that we may have a complete collection of all the ceremonies that accompany the forked creature from the cradle to the grave.' Originally Talbot had mistaken Colley for the ship's chaplain and had unthinkingly observed to Cumbershum that 'it was fortunate we had a chaplain to perform all the other rites, from the first to the last.' Cumbershum's reaction was to choke over his drink.

This is the first occasion on which the word 'rite' is used in the novel. here it has reference to the Christian ceremonies that accompany important human events. But the second time it occurs is in a very different, indeed in an essentially secular context: this time it describes not a Christian ceremony, but the complicated set of procedures demanded for the naval exercise known as 'shooting the sun'. This whole operation, in which the midshipmen hold the brass triangles of their theodolites to their faces to take a bearing, is accorded by 'the common sort' who witness it 'a respect such as they might have paid to the solemnest moment of a religious service . . .

the glittering instruments were their Mumbo Jumbo.' Talbot
had previously asked Cumbershum how the seamen, notor-
iously superstitious, managed without religious services,
expressing his question in terms of the same phrase: 'Do you
not require the occasional invocation of Mumbo Jumbo?'
Obviously they practise an alternative version. Though Talbot might inwardly put the case for Galileo, Copernicus and
Kepler, it is clear that the Royal Navy still operates from older
principles – the 'customs of the service'. According to such
customs, the sun still 'climbs up the sky', whatever the learned
might say. And these customs are supported and interpreted
by a document whose authority has all the force of holy writ
for the seamen – the Captain's Standing Orders, in which are
inscribed all the rites, practices and taboos relating to ship
procedure.

It is Colley's misfortune not to understand or heed such
ancient customs of the sea. But worse still, he is the representative of the Christian rites that the pagan seamen have
rejected. As a result he is cast in the role of scapegoat in that
other notorious rite of passage, the crossing-the-line ceremony. Thematically, his being dragged out of his cabin
before King Neptune for judgement and subsequent humiliation may be compared to the persecution and murder of
Pangall in *The Spire*. But there is a significant difference, even
a reversal involved. Metaphorically, Pangall's kingdom which
fell before the invaders was the old pagan world succumbing
to Christianity. In *Rites of Passage* it is the other way round.
The rituals of the established Church are here made to give
way before pagan customs that seize on the Church's representative as their appropriate victim; what we witness here is
the moment of transition from a predominantly Christian
community to a secular society, inspired by eighteenth-
century free-thinkers, a society which we ourselves have inher-
ited. Judged from yet another viewpoint, however, the godless
masons and sailors are not so very different, versions of the
blood-sacrificing heathens from whom the Israelites were so

anxious to distinguish themselves (as Colley's biblical *sortes* suggested). What is at stake both in this novel and in *Darkness Visible* is the validity of the Christian myth itself. It is characteristic of Golding's complexity that he should come up with two opposing views of Colley's death – it can be regarded both as a victory and as a defeat. It is a defeat in the sense that among the sailors he abandoned all claim to spiritual authority and allowed his office to be publicly disgraced, as well as in a further theological sense: as Summers explains 'he knows nothing of his own religion . . . I take it upon myself as a Christian . . . to aver that a Christian *cannot* despair!' Yet it is a triumph in the sense that Colley sacrifices himself to an ideal of priestly duty higher than himself, and one unattainable by him. A sceptic like Talbot would never have been capable of such an act which could be felt, in some mysterious way, to redeem Colley, if only from the moral stupidity of his fellow-passengers. Because he is the representative of the Christian Church Colley's isolation becomes more and more complete as the voyage proceeds. The only show of devotion he inspires is in Zenobia – a show that prompts Talbot to remark that 'a chain of tawdry linked them both.' Talbot himself admits to being glad to be free 'from the whole paraphernalia of Established Religion', only going to Colley's service to spite Captain Anderson, because he does not 'choose to submit to tyranny'. As for Captain Anderson, like Captain Cook before him he would 'as soon have taken the plague into his ship as a parson'. His rejection of what Colley stands for is total.

There is, then, something about the ship and its passengers and crew as a whole which seems alien, even hostile to everything that Colley represents – the militant atheism of Mr Prettiman, the politic faith of Talbot (who regards the Church as a buttress of social order), the sinister character of the purser and his underworld domain, and the quite unreasonable hatred of Captain Anderson. Deverel later explains the reason for his hatred, in a kind of postscript: Anderson is the illegitimate son of an aristocrat, whose mistress, Anderson's mother, was hastily married off to the family tutor, now promoted to the ranks of the clergy by the gift of a living. Anderson's step or supposed father had thus been a clergyman. No wonder Deverel was convulsed with laughter, and thought 'the coincidence . . . past the wit of man to invent' when he learnt of Talbot's absurd scheme to marry Zenobia off to Colley if she turned out to be pregnant. In Anderson's pathological hatred of Colley and all he stands for, there is more than a hint of the ruined Adam. This is made explicit in the incident when Talbot is invited to his cabin and finds himself in the Captain's 'private paradise', surrounded by climbing plants which Anderson lovingly cultivates. As Talbot comments 'perhaps the stormy or sullen face with which he was wont to leave his paradise was that of the expelled Adam.' There is certainly no sign in his attitude towards established religion as represented by Colley that Anderson is nurturing his garland plants to lay at the feet of his Maker. Rather, it seems, the memory of a lost paradise that he takes with him on deck changes him from a ruined Adam to another exile from a blessed state – Satan himself. According to Milton, Satan remained 'not less than Archangel ruined' though banished from the delights of Heaven, commanding a court at least powerful enough to prove him a worthy adversary of God. Anderson similarly is 'king or emperor' of his 'floating society, with prerogatives of justice and mercy'. On shipboard the Captain is empowered to conduct marriages and funerals, as if he too were a minister, and empowered to investigate Colley's death as if he were a Justice of the Peace. It is through his surrogates and with his licence that a travesty of judgement is meted out to the pathetic representative of the Christian Church. This incident in which Colley is brought before the pagan god Neptune to be judged, condemned and punished is central to the book's theme, a parodic version of the central preoccupation of *Darkness Visible*. Just before the baiting of the crossing-the-line ceremony, Colley experiences an apocalyptic vision that mysteriously warns him, as his servant Phillips had tried to do, of the judgement to follow. Yet it only succeeds in making the advent of its arresting officers the more terrifying, because somehow expected:

> What I saw as I stood, petrified as it were, will be stamped on my mind till my dying day. *Our* end of the ship – the two raised portions at the back – was crowded with passengers and officers, all silent and all staring forward over my head . . . Our huge ship was motionless and her sails still hung down. On her right hand the red sun was setting and on her left the full moon was rising, the one directly across from the other . . . Here plainly to be seen were the very scales of GOD.
>
> The scales tilted, the double light faded and we were wrought of ivory and ebony by the moon. The people moved about forward and hung lanterns by the dozen from the rigging, so that I saw now that they had erected something like a bishop's *cathedra* beyond the ungainly paunch of tarpaulin. I began to understand. I began to tremble. I was alone! Yes, in that vast ship with her numberless souls I was alone in a place where on a sudden I feared the Justice of GOD unmitigated by HIS Mercy! On a sudden I dreaded both GOD and man!

It may be Zenobia who first quotes from Coleridge's *Ancient Mariner* –

> Alone, alone, all, all alone.
> Alone on a wide wide sea!

but it is in Colley's journal that these words find their most passionate echo, just as he intuitively echoes Coleridge's treatment of the alternating sun and moon as symbols, respectively, of God's Justice and of His Mercy, though in the poem they are never seen together in the sky or explicitly represented in terms of divine scales, as here. Like the Mariner, Colley, through an infraction of the sailors' rules, becomes

their scapegoat. In the moment of isolation before his doom
begins, Colley fears not merely the 'horrid ceremonies' of
which he guesses himself to be the intended victim, but that
during the process he and his religion will be weighed in the
balance of those dreadful scales and found wanting.

And this is precisely what happens. Though part of his
mind knows that, when he is called 'to appear before the
throne', the words are mere 'foolery', he recognises that,
behind the foolery, more powerful forces are at work, that the
laughter around him is in a very real sense 'demonic', that his
captors are 'hot with the devil's brew', that the three-pronged
fork of Neptune is really the devil's fork, that Apocalypse is
nigh and Hell gapes before him. Colley's fear of the Justice of
God unmitigated by His Mercy is inspired by something more
than a sense of his own personal failure since, when he comes
to himself after the ceremony is over, he feels only his own
'renewed certainties of the Great Truths of the Christian
Religion'. It is, he recognises, these great truths which are
being tried and tested, weighed in the balance and which at
all costs must be upheld in the face of all the legions of hell.
Dressed, therefore, in all the finery of the Church and carrying
with him his lordship's license as a sort of talisman (as Aeneas
carried the golden bough, or Matty his wooden Bible) Colley
goes out to rejoin battle with the Captain and to defend his
Master's honour.

His preoccupation with the clothes of his calling and the
respect due to them is, at one level, simply a reflection of the
parson's personal inadequacy; but there is an interesting
exchange when he approaches the Captain to demand an
apology which suggests that more than Colley's reputation is
at stake:

'You have your uniform, Captain Anderson, and I have
mine. I shall approach them in that garb, those orna-
ments of the Spiritual Man!'
'Uniform!'

'You do not understand, sir? I shall go to them in those garments which my long studies and ordination enjoin on me.'

If Colley is right in his awful realisation that 'I was the foe!', this last conflict in which he engages must be seen as one enacted between Established Religion and the pagan gods of the navy, both flying their respective colours and distinguished by their dress. It is an unequal conflict since Colley is ranged not only against the officers, who ought to have been susceptible to old-fashioned notions of fair play, but against the common sailors who, uninhibited by any such niceties, expose him, and in so doing destroy him as surely as the workmen in *The Spire* destroyed Pangall.

In *Rites of Passage*, however, there is no positive implicit in his destruction, and the reversal whereby the forces of darkness and ignorance are triumphant means that the novel is darker in its implications than *The Spire* had been. The inner message is that the forces of paganism sometimes overcome, perhaps *have* overcome in a wider historical perspective, since our own society pays no more respect to its clergy than the ship's crew and passengers pay to Colley. But such undertones are largely offset by a prevailing note of tough-minded, earthy comedy whose effect is partly to divert attention from the book's deeper mysteries. It is nevertheless on a note of mystery that it ends, with the disappearance of one of the minor characters, the 'limping old fellow', the walking Falconer, who dispenses homespun wisdom as readily as paregoric, the 'omniscient, ubiquitous Wheeler'. He is the ship's know-all who acts as the Captain's informer and is presumably pushed overboard for peaching on Billy Rogers, perhaps by Billy Rogers himself. But he is much more than this, as Talbot half guesses when he finds Wheeler, and not Colley's own man, Phillips, standing guard over the corpse with a 'lighted face' and what Talbot can only describe as an 'expression of positive saintliness'. Since Talbot had to disci-

pline himself to resist his paregoric, the opium compound
bringing fantasy and oblivion which Wheeler so readily
offered, we are left wondering whether the same consolation
had been afforded to Colley. And if so, whether this had
affected his actions, even his manner of expressing himself –
after all, it had influenced and darkened Coleridge's vision.
Perhaps, like Evelyn de Tracy in *The Pyramid*, Wheeler had all
along been playing the much more important part of Mephistopheles in this strange drama of shipboard life, catering to all
men's desires, revealing to them the darkness of their hearts,
and finally claiming them for his own. When Wheeler
vanishes, it is after all only inferred that he has fallen or been
pushed overboard:

> He *was* being sought. Summers has just told me. The
> man has disappeared. He has fallen overboard. Wheeler!
> He has gone like a dream, with his puffs of white hair, and
> his shining baldness, his *sanctified* smile, his complete
> knowledge of everything that goes on in a ship, his pare-
> goric, and his willingness to obtain for a gentleman any-
> thing in the wide, wide world, provided the gentleman
> pays for it!

There is certainly a Mephistophelean ring about that 'willing-
ness to obtain for a gentleman anything in the wide, wide
world, provided the gentleman pays for it'. Is it merely an
accident that so soon after his disappearance, when the passengers are considering what play to perform, Miss Granham
mentions the possibility of 'the play *Faust* by the German
author Goethe'? His purpose apparently fulfilled, Wheeler has
vanished *like a dream*. The image is highly appropriate. All
along Talbot has been nagged by the thought that *'Plato was
right'*, that even though Plato contradicts the common-sense
view of the world to which he is temperamentally inclined, the
edges between appearance and reality have nevertheless
become impossibly blurred. The unreal ship on the unreal

ocean on its unreal voyage has tilted his whole moral spectrum, leaving him uncertain as to where the ship's drama
ends and real life begins. It is this that prompts the disturbing
statement with which the book ends:

> With lack of sleep and too much understanding I grow a
> little crazy, I think, like all men at sea who live too close
> to each other and too close thereby to all that is mon-
> strous under the sun and moon.

The voyage as a metaphor for life itself is one of the oldest
and most powerful of images, going back at least to the
Odyssey. Existence can be seen as a passage, bounded only by
the terminal certainties of unbeing – certainties in that they
are all we can be sure of, but of which we can know nothing.
Something of this condition is momentarily grasped by Colley
when he asks the navigator Mr Smiles how deep the waters
are, and after an enigmatic 'Who can say?' is told that they
may be a mile, even two miles deep: 'I was almost overcome
with faintness. Here we are, suspended between the land
below the waters and the sky like a nut on a branch or a leaf
on a pond!' To be suspended between solid ground and sky is
the characteristic transitional position in traditional rites of
passage, imitated by ceremonies in which the subject is carried and not allowed to set his foot on the ground. In Arnold
Van Gennep's classic account of *The Rites of Passage*, he begins
by describing the rites in territorial terms, explaining that,
as certain boundaries are endowed with significance, they
can usually be described by metaphors of position, and symbolised by the traversing of certain demarcated areas. In
terms of the novel, these limits are very clearly delineated.
The Captain's right to occupy his quarterdeck without intrusion makes it 'the Sacred Precincts' for Talbot. The white line
across the deck is another such boundary. Talbot's cabin,
which seems to him merely a 'hutch', is – significantly –
opposite and equivalent to Colley's. Both young men start

from the same position, physically speaking, in the ship. Both are of an age, socially aspiring, both must pass through the rites of passage to manhood, yet one succeeds and the other fails, as if there were a competition for a place which only one can win. Their rivalry has elements of the conflict between Oliver and Bobby Ewan, grammar school lad versus public school boy, but the outcome is potentially tragic and there is more than a hint that Talbot succeeds at the cost of his rival's death.

From the first their lives seem bound up together and they have more in common than Talbot cares to admit. But it is Lieutenant Summers who brings home to Talbot just how far responsibility for Colley's death lies at his door. When Talbot so thoughtlessly invaded the Captain's quarterdeck, he was gratified to see Anderson swallow his anger at the mention of Talbot's influential patron; but Anderson took his temper out on the defenceless Colley. As Summers explains, he 'continued to humiliate *him* because he could not humiliate *you*'. It was Talbot who made Colley a further object of the Captain's anger when he urged him to conduct a service for the passengers, not because he liked or felt the need of religious services, but as a move in the power conflict developing between himself and Anderson: 'The brooding captain should not dictate to me in this manner! What! Is *he* to tell *me* whether I should have a service to attend or not?' Again, Colley bears the brunt of a resentment that would more appropriately be directed against Talbot, so that Anderson allows Colley to be chosen as the victim of the 'badger bag'. Talbot was the only man on board not present on this occasion because he had seized the opportunity to relieve his lust for Zenobia. He was also the only man who might effectively have protested 'at that childish savagery', as he finally admits. Colley bores and irritates him, so he avoids him, becoming a guilty bystander as Colley makes a final spectacle of himself. When Summers appeals to him to intervene because Colley is dying, his response is still complacent and his efforts too little and too late. He cannot speak to Colley in any language that the parson can understand (the book includes more than one reference to the impossibility of successfully translating one language into another). Golding has explained that Talbot was necessary as an onlooker, 'and it seemed natural that, in a subtle way, Colley should be killed by Talbot. That, of course, is a subtlety beyond a subtlety, since it's a series of levers from Talbot that kills Colley.'[10] Lieutenant Summers, exemplar of the honest man, makes the same point in the course of the novel: '*You* are the man most responsible.' Talbot's final determination to make some financial provision for Colley's sister suggests that he accepts that accusation as containing at least an element of truth.

In describing the rites of passage, Van Gennep divided them into three main stages – separation, transition and incorporation. Both young men seem to pass through these phases as they first take their leave – Talbot from his parents and brothers, Colley from his sister. In the transitional phase, they struggle to come to terms with life on shipboard – in physical terms, as they attempt, at first unsuccessfully, to cope with the ship's motion, and then in other ways, as they try to discover their position within the new social pyramid. But it is the act of incorporation that assumes the greatest importance, the moment of full acceptance into a new society or phase of life, the symbolic completion of the process of transition. Commonly it entails a sharing of food with the new group as a gesture of community with them, but it may also involve sexual, sometimes homosexual acts. Talbot's incorporation may be regarded as complete when he enjoys a meal of marrow bones at the Captain's table. This scene, one of high comedy, takes place as Colley dies, isolated and rejected in his cabin, a death that is in part the consequence of his failure to perform society's unspecified rites correctly. Colley too undergoes a rite of incorporation but if that of Talbot is positive, and socially speaking an ascent, that of Colley is negative and involves a descent, back to the level from which he had so

laboriously elevated himself. In fact Colley may be said to
undergo two acts of incorporation, the first as part of the
crossing-the-line ceremonies when he is baptised, not in holy
water but with human ordure, a nauseous warning that he,
like the whole tribe of fallen man, is 'a low, filthy fellow', the
dirt that loves dirt. And the baptism by filth is followed by a
travestied rite of communion, the participation required by
the incorporation rite becoming the act of *fellatio*. He kneels
not before the Host but before the handsome Billy Rogers in
an act of perverse worship.

This whole uncomfortably blasphemous episode can be
minimised or dismissed – Talbot refers to it as a 'ridiculous
schoolboy trick'. Yet unaccountably its effect on Colley is very
different: 'Joy! Joy! Joy!' he announces, and his immediate
reaction is starkly contrasted with Talbot's reaction after his
loveless, if more 'adult', copulation with Zenobia – 'irritation . . . subsumed into a kind of universal sadness'. Before
he descends into the cabin locker with the misguided intention
of reprimanding the sailors, Colley's testament ends – on a
note of Coleridgean joy very different from the note of terror
he felt on seeing the divine scales of the sun and moon in the
sky, just before the 'badger bag'. For Coleridge, joy was not
simply a heightened happiness; it was an experience in which
feelings were linked in a fruitful and outgoing impulse of love
to all living things, the loss of which forms the subject of his
'Dejection Ode'. It is exactly this spontaneous surge of joy that
releases the Ancient Mariner from his spiritual isolation, en-
abling him to bless the sea-serpents and initiating his progress towards redemption, as the albatross falls from his neck
and he finds he can pray again:

> Within the shadow of the ship
> I watched their rich attire:
> Blue, glossy green, and velvet black,
> They coiled and swam; and every track
> Was a flash of golden fire.

> O happy living things! no tongue
> Their beauty might declare:
> A spring of love gushed from my heart,
> And I blessed them unaware:

Colley's last words are a prosaic paraphrase of this wonderful moment, but irradiated by very much the same impulse of love towards all living things, as he descends to the cable locker and the ambivalent act of worship before Billy Rogers:

> I gazed down into the water, the blue, the green, the purple, the snowy, sliding foam! I saw with a new feeling of security the long, green weed that wavers under the water from our wooden sides. There was, it seemed too, a peculiar richness in the columns of our rounded sails . . . It seemed to me then – it still seems so – that I was and am consumed by a great love of all things, the sea, the ship, the sky, the gentlemen and the people and of course OUR REDEEMER above all! . . . ALL THINGS PRAISE HIM!

Like Mr Pedigree in *Darkness Visible*, Colley is motivated by a selfless impulse of love for human beauty which is at once rare and real enough. Like Evie in the *Pyramid*, Colley breaks all the stifling taboos of his society, at first accidentally and then, to some extent, intentionally. Like Bounce, he is destroyed by the society whose rules he has overturned. There remains a central mystery about Colley's joyous and intolerable act of love and degradation. It is

> The awful daring of a moment's surrender
> Which an age of prudence can never retract
> By this, and this only, we have existed

Such a moment occurs at a point where extremes meet, where transcendent joy in beauty touches the gnawing shame and terror of society's rejection, the moment of the black springing bough among the apple blossom or the kingfisher's flight across the panicshot darkness of the water.

6

The Paper Men
(1984)

Golding's three most recent novels can be seen as a kind of triptych, with *Rites of Passage* at the centre, not only chronologically, but also because it was the most enthusiastically received, being more concerned than the other two (for all its historical setting) with everyday life, the 'ordinary universe' in which most people live most of the time. It is thus the easiest of the three to place and keep in focus. Yet in different ways and to varying degrees, all three novels testify to spiritual truths that have no obvious part in the daily round. The less favourable reactions to *Darkness Visible* (widely acknowledged as a major novel, but a difficult one) and the largely unfavourable reception of *The Paper Men* (judged distinctly minor) seem directly related to the degree of tact with which Golding presents the manifestation of spiritual forces to a largely sceptical readership. In each of these books individuals bear witness, often setting down their experiences in journals or records of some kind, but in each the credence we are required to accord their documents varies, demanding more or less active levels of acquiescence. Matty describes his encounters with brightly-clothed spirits, but his naive goodness is balanced against Sophy's hyper-intelligent evil, and both are counteracted by the intelligent mediocrities, Sim and Edwin, who remain closest to the reader's experience and with whose responses the book ends. This tripartite structure of *Darkness*

Visible is followed by the double perspective of *Rites of Passage*, where Colley's passionate responses to the spiritual world are mediated through the cheerfully prosaic scepticism of Talbot; his temperamental preference for reductive explanations tends to insulate the reader from having to accept unmodified symbolic or supernatural interpretations. But *The Paper Men* affords only one point of view, a single witness and one far less attractive in every way than Talbot who, though young and arrogant, was also responsive and deeply interested in the human world around him. The narrator of *The Paper Men* is old, callous and self-absorbed; at the same time the experiences of the spiritual world that he records are more direct and bizarre than anything that takes place in *Rites of Passage*. Disconcertingly, this narrator sounds and looks all too like his creator – Bill Golding metamorphosed into Wilf Barclay, an ageing novelist who had served in the navy during the war and whose earliest books had found immediate success, selling well enough to ensure him a permanent income (the first is entitled *Coldharbour*, for the significance of which see above, p. 50, and note 4 to chapter 1). Barclay has a straggly white beard and is irritated at finding himself the subject of an academic 'light industry'. He prefers to regard himself as a 'moving target', eluding his critics' boss shots. *The Paper Men* is in some sense his autobiography, and one of Barclay's motives in writing it is to be revenged upon his would-be biographer:

> Think Rick – all the people who get lice like you in their hair, all the people spied on, followed, lied about, all the people offered up to the great public – we'll be revenged, Rick, I'll be revenged on the whole lot of them . . .

Of course such similarities are no more than traps for critical heffalumps, a form of crossed fingers that should avert further odious comparisons more than they invite them. Barclay resembles his creator only in his most public, that is to say his most superficial aspects. But at first these resemblances tended to deflect attention from the kind of novel that Golding had actually written, rather as Prufrock's resemblance to T.S. Eliot has sometimes hindered his Love Song from being approached as a dramatic monologue. The strictly limited viewpoint of *The Paper Men* requires us to understand what has really happened not only through what we are told, but also through what we are *not* told, to reconstruct events in the light of the narrator's narrowed vision. Thus it should take its place in the tradition of novels such as Henry James's *What Maisie Knew* or Ford Madox Ford's *The Good Soldier*, novels where the narrator's naive perceptions, whether the result of innocence or ignorance, only provide a part of the story. The rest must be pieced together by the reader out of his superior experience or understanding. But in both these examples the narrators' limitations lie in their inability to grasp the nature of sexual passion, a knowledge that adult readers can usually supply without difficulty. Golding in *The Paper Men* has created a narrator who is a man of exceptional intelligence of a worldly kind, but is morally and spiritually stupid. He is adrift in a universe of numinous forces, and we must identify his failure to understand or come to terms with that universe. Like T.S. Eliot, Golding does not want to hear

> Of the wisdom of old men, but rather of their folly,
> Their fear of fear and frenzy, their fear of possession,
> Of belonging to another, or to others, or to God.

Barclay, the narrator, is 'suggestible', attuned to receiving mystically transmitted messages, yet unable to interpret them except in so far as they correspond to his own view of things, so correct interpretation is left to the reader who may be hardly better placed for the task. Repelled by Barclay's character and largely unprepared for or unequipped to take in the wider theological perspectives that Barclay's solipsism denies him, we are in danger of being baffled, confused and disappointed.[1]

If one major problem lies in the unreliable narrator, whose account of events requires adjustment or reinterpretation, another lies in the continuous shifting between literal and symbolic levels, between familiar stereotypes and their subversion, between dream and reality – and often the symbolic level, the subverted stereotype, the dream, seem to be of greater importance. An outline of the main events can reveal some of their underlying implications, but taken as a whole the book has a tendency to elude consistent critical interpretations, and this may well be exactly what Golding intended. After all, it is centrally concerned with a critic's clumsy attempts to pin down a writer on the printed pages of his projected biography. This attempt is so energetically and effectively foiled that the critic is finally forced to silence his subject, to reduce him to the status of an object by shooting him. Faced with such a theme it would be peculiarly arrogant for anyone to believe that it might all be summed up neatly, that one might pluck out the heart of Golding's mystery.

The story has a circular movement, ending where it began, at Wilf Barclay's secluded English country house. The opening and closing pages provide a pattern of reversal that characterises the structure at every level. During the rest of the book, Barclay travels across Europe, driven on as if by demons or in flight from God – a flying Dutchman or a wandering Jew. He is pursued by his aspiring biographer Rick Tucker, an unwelcome reminder of what he has been and is, and beyond Tucker by his master, the mysterious Halliday. He returns from his voyage of discovery having been forced to acknowledge the existence of God, yet the God he finds is formed in his own image, encased in a rigid structure, its eyes burning; it shares his intolerance and regards him as its chosen comic victim. Barclay's existential sense of his own absurdity is thus delicately balanced against his sense of personal and predestined damnation. His discovery of something beyond himself which is an infinite repetition of his finite self may be compared to Sophy's – for both of them, it involves an inversion of Christian values, an 'Evil be thou my good.' Yet whereas Sophy actively promoted evil, Barclay mainly acquiesces in it. So intensely self-absorbed, solipsistic, so Berkeleian, perhaps, is his conception of the universe that the God he finds there may hunt him down, but having insisted upon existence, seems powerless to change him. His sins remain those of omission, deadlier because more trivial than those of commission. A further vision reveals God not as an extension of himself, but as total Otherness, a blessed state which Barclay terms 'isness' or (more technically) *Istigkeit;* again its impact on him seems negligible.

Barclay is bankrupt not only morally, but artistically. He cannot change because he has become a hollow man, a man encased in the staitjacket of what Golding has called 'literary mummification',[2] and with little left inside his shell. But in a society that is more concerned with the superficies, with image rather than reality, a society whose sacred speakers have become scarcely more than so many gas-filled balloons, it is hard to retain individuality or integrity. In some sense Barclay is the product of the corruption of his times, the man of his moment. It is not merely that late twentieth-century society pays scant attention to the truths of revealed religion; far worse, it seems to have reversed Christian moral values, so that sin is considered more exciting, interesting and life-enhancing than the inhibitions and rejections that necessarily accompany virtue. As Sophy had done, this society has discovered the ultimate thrill of hyper-violence or outrage. Near the end of *The Paper Men,* the sophisticates of Barclay's London club jokingly propose two modern pieces of statuary to correspond to the club's Victorian statue of Psyche, an idealised and ethereal image of the soul. These new and more appropriate icons for our times will represent characteristic forms of outrage – an act of incest (to illustrate 'mother-fucker' in bronze) and one of homosexuality (to illustrate 'Johnny's penetration' in 'white marble, for purity'). This is the society that has made itself a false religion from paper and print, complete

with its own literary idols. As part of its ritual, certain writers
are elected to the status of secular saints and canonised for
their energetic pursuit of experience. The more they sin, the
more actively they indulge in alcohol, women and vice, the
closer they come to the ideal of the artist as martyr, suffering
an artificial passion for the sake of their art. Within the terms
of this absurd and alarming travesty of Christianity Barclay
discovers that he bears the stigmata, sign of his true election
as a paper saint; he will eventually die from the fifth wound of
Christ, a wound inflicted by the bullet of his thwarted and
vengeful biographer.

At one level, Barclay's stigmata reflect how suggestible he
is, something that his experience of being hypnotised had
confirmed. This trait is obviously connected with his sensitivity as a writer, and if we are to accept Golding's suggestion,
may even indicate a lost potential for genuine sainthood: great
novelists, Golding believes, may be people who possess a
special kind of awareness, a kind of sixth sense, 'a tincture of
that quality which exists in full power among the saints'.[3]
This must seem almost paradoxical, given the modern view of
the novelist as a man sanctified by his sins. Yet, though from
one point of view Barclay's stigmata seem purely ironic, from
another, they may be a measure of his self-betrayal, of gifts
thrown away, their pain the pain of a vocation disappointed or
unfulfilled.

Barclay himself finally comes to regard his stigmata as the
last and most theologically witty of a long series of practical
jokes played on him by God or providence. He had thought of
them as indicating some form of election, until the vicar had
commented acidly, 'You must be very proud of them . . . After
all there were three crosses.' Yet these dismissive words bring
Barclay not disappointment, but relief – 'the peace and security of knowing myself a thief'. From another, and very different point of view, perhaps all writers are in some sense thieves,
the best among them those who steal down fire from heaven.
The pains in his hands certainly seem linked with the guilt of

being a writer: at one point he admits 'my writing hand hurt like the devil.' And if Barclay has received his stigmata, spiritually speaking, 'for cowardice in the face of the enemy', a similar charge may be made on artistic grounds. His earliest novels had not merely been successful, but 'There were things, mantic moments, certainties, if you like, whole episodes that had blazed, hurt, been suffered for.' Yet these had all been wasted on his readers. The critics, eagerly engaged in dissecting books into so many separate pieces, or disintegrating their sources, failed to recognise these moments, and now Barclay is content to write with less effort and more economy: 'I did not need to invent, to dive, suffer, endure that obscurely necessary anguish in the pursuit of the – unreadable.' He finds that books may be made by manipulating reality, fantasising around what he knows or desires. Indeed, he has little alternative, since by this stage he has irreversibly withdrawn from any involvement in or engagement with the world around him. Barclay's main moral defect thus becomes his main artistic defect, and since he is the ostensible author of *The Paper Men*, the reader is faced with the problem that Golding's success in presenting the withdrawn and self-absorbed world of his hero, in recreating this mimetically from within, risks undermining the book's appeal.

Golding has never, perhaps, fully allowed for the extent to which readers identify, or try to identify, with a novel's main character. He was understandably disappointed when they sympathised too readily with the depraved Pincher Martin in his struggle against the inevitable, and when they felt limited by Oliver's narrow outlook in *The Pyramid*. Yet both novels evinced their author's total commitment, his power to identify himself wholly with his own creations, to imitate their way of seeing and experiencing so completely that, in so doing, he created a further set of artistic problems for himself. In *The Paper Men* problems of this kind are well to the fore, and certainly contributed to the book's cool reception. The portrait of Barclay, in one sense a triumph in its accurate depiction of an egoism subordinating all experience to itself, is, in another sense, only too accurate, only too successful. An artist of self-effacing integrity has brilliantly reproduced a bad artist writing a bad book in bad faith – for Barclay's primary motive in writing his account is to anticipate and so frustrate his would-be biographer. Negative capability here proves something of a liability.

Barclay, then, is a false saint as he is a failed artist, a Judas to all that he most values, but the book tacitly recognises the gap between achievement and public acclaim, a gap which may disturb the best as well as the worst of writers. T.S. Eliot, assessing the gifts reserved for age that 'set a crown upon your lifetime's effort' recognised that 'fools' approval stings and honour stains.' Literary canonisation is achieved, among other things, in terms of literary prizes. It cannot be entirely an accident that Golding published *The Paper Men* fresh from the triumph of the Booker prize awarded to *Rites of Passage* (Barclay discourses to Tucker on rites of passage at one point), and only a few months after he received the Nobel prize for literature, late in 1983. His latest novel might indeed be read as a passionate repudiation of a system that wants to elevate writers to a kind of priesthood, to find in their flawed gospels and the oracles of their interviews keys to the universe, or instructions for us all to live by. If so, it is a rejection of success in the very mode by which he has achieved it, a refusal of complacency, of his status as a fossilised 'great' novelist, comparable to similar refusals by other major modern writers who have felt alarmed at finding themselves idolised, and elevated to institutional status. Yet however reluctant Golding is to participate, the juggernaut of adulation grinds on, its attendant academics fight for such latter-day relics as corrected manuscripts or page-proofs, rejected fragments, diaries, letters, any evidence that will advance the hagiographer's detailed record of a writer's follies and failings – the sins that guarantee his martyrdom genuine, that safely proclaim him a saint in the canons of literature.

As befits a paper man, Barclay has carefully hoarded everything he has ever written;[4] he has left the fullest evidence of himself in endless fragments of paper, sticky not merely with butter or marmalade from the dustbin, but also with the guilt or shame of the sordid events they record. The accumulating words pile up not only in his printed works, but in boxes in his house (from time to time his wife send telegrams asking him to take them away), within the bound covers of his journal and, after he has lost this, 'in telephone books or on walls or the windows of cars or lavatory paper'. He has also left love letters, including the obscene ones he wrote to the only woman who refused him, letters that a bent lawyer failed to retrieve. But the incriminating documents stacked up against him are by no means all his own work, though the theme of the artist's pride and self-betrayal seems as important here as it had been in *The Spire*. There are other love letters written to him, like the fragments of Lucinda's which, salvaged from the dustbin, cost him his marriage. There is the unpublished manuscript once submitted to him from which he pinched the only promising idea. There are also photographs, obscene ones taken by the lubricious Lucinda with her instant camera, as well as the snap taken by Tucker which Barclay later rediscovers hanging in the Swiss hotel bar. Inside the camera that Tucker always carries with him is a tape recorder, so that their conversations are all on record. These, with much other material, have reverted to the possession of Halliday, the mysterious American billionaire, banker and ardent collector of all the relics and records of *literati* – a spiritual accountant as sinister and elusive as the purser in *Rites of Passage*. Like all gods, Halliday has his benevolent aspect. He has endowed the University of Astrakhan with 'the ecumenical temple, the skijump and the snow machine and the courts for real tennis', but he is also keen in pursuit of his prey, and as Barclay realises how much of his essence Halliday already possesses, he begins to feel that resistance is vain, becoming almost reconciled to the persecution of this ubiquitous deity. Indeed,

Halliday becomes scarcely separable from the infernal God who has pursued Barclay to an unavoidable confrontation, and the bleak recognition of where he is:

> 'Why, this is Hell, nor am I out of it.'
> 'I. am. sin.'

Yet though Barclay echoes the words of Marlowe's Mephistopheles, his role in the fable is rather that of Faustus, and it is Halliday's agent Rick Tucker who has been cast as Mephistopheles. This young academic with his pretended professorship and dubious credentials hopes to assure his own future by becoming 'the Barclay man'. He 'badgers' or 'dogs' Barclay – indeed he is initially taken for a badger as he rifles through the dustbin for cast-off relics. Tucker then tempts Barclay's vanity, urging him to sign a contract, an updated version of the traditional pact that will confer sole rights over Barclay's literary soul, giving unlimited access to his manuscripts and permission to write his official biography. In return Barclay is offered immortality as a plaster saint with an established niche in 'the great Pageant of English Literature'. Barclay shies away from this peculiar version of immortality for a number of reasons, not least among them a natural and understandable resentment at such blatant prying into his private life. But he feels other and deeper anxieties: to yield to Tucker's demand would be to have his actions called to account, to be summoned to a premature judgement which he cannot yet face. He is only too conscious of how sordid and contemptible his past would appear, and guiltily fears that Tucker might be able to unearth its buried secrets – such as having killed an Indian in a hit-and-run accident in South America – as if he were the all-seeing eye of God. He knows too that just as he is no longer prepared to pay the price necessary to create a work of art, so he cannot pretend to measure up to the level of excess required to give him the appropriate romantic stature. His wife Elizabeth perceptively taunts him with wanting to act the genius, to play the great man, while at the same time remaining a popular writer:

> That's what you always wanted, Wilf . . . the sacré monster outside the accepted rules, a national treasure, the point about you being words that the world would not willingly let die . . .

Yet Barclay lacks conviction even in this. He has neither the artist's passion nor his self-surrender. Everyone assumes that he is enacting this self-squandering role – 'boozing, wenching, living it up' – when in fact he passes most of his time in absorbed self-contemplation. If Barclay is Faust, he is a Faust who refuses to sell a soul spotted with petty and largely incidental sins; who refuses Helen, perhaps from the fear of self-commitment; and who systematically tempts, frustrates and defeats his tempter. Tucker is the devil who makes an ass of himself and finally finds himself outwitted by the superior cunning of his victim.

Tucker is also the book's second 'paper man', the aspiring Boswell to Barclay's Johnson. As Barclay depends for his living on the success of his novels, Tucker depends on Barclay's co-operation, and is thus his parasite; each is determined to survive at the expense of the other. The book is structured as a complex duel between them, with Tucker as the hairy Esau and Barclay the smooth Jacob, stealing a march on his brother, and perhaps even depriving him of his blessing, his peace of mind or his luck as well. Certainly by the end of the book Tucker has lost all these things, and also forfeited Mary Lou; he dangles with good luck charms which he hopes, possibly believes, will reverse this downward spiral. At first Barclay seemed to be pursued, even hunted down by the American, but as something altogether more powerful than Tucker forces itself into Barclay's field of awareness, so he changes; turning on his tormentor, he seems intent on destroying him, perhaps because he is the only human being left over whom he has any power. For Tucker worships at Barclay's shrine even though he is obscurely gratified by his idol's feet of clay. Johnny's suggestion that Barclay needs a chum, perhaps a dog, determines Barclay that Tucker must play out the part that his doggedness and uncritical admiration cut him out for; and he will die like the dog he is. Now their roles are reversed: Tucker also experiences paranoia, believing that he sees his master, waving the commission, in places Barclay has never in fact visited – just as Barclay had apparently imagined Tucker dogging his footsteps across Europe. As if Tucker were now Faust, time is running out for him, for the implacable Halliday has allowed him seven years in which to pull off the deal.

The contrast between the book's opening and closing scenes is designed to reveal the extent of their role-reversal. In the first scene Barclay discovers Tucker rifling his dustbin and accidentally shoots him with his airgun. Broad farce follows as he pulls Tucker's robe off to look for the wound he has inflicted; at the same time his own pyjama trousers fall down. Then his wife appears and unluckily picks up a fragment of an old love letter that has adhered to Tucker during his researches in the dustbin. The book ends with further undignified struggles between Barclay and Tucker: they fight at the Random Club where the air is filled with yet more detritus of the paper world: 'menus, wine lists, order books, bits of manuscript flew up into the air and seemed to float like snow.' Barclay makes a final effort to write his autobiography and destroy all the accumulated relics of his paper lifetime on a massive bonfire, while Tucker, his sanity finally snapped, prepares to shoot him.

In his depiction of Tucker, Golding has allowed himself to vent a certain amount of spleen against American academe of the kind Philip Larkin's sharp little poem 'Posterity' had voiced; here the poet is reduced to a research topic allotted to a reluctant Jewish student, Jake Balokowski. Curiously, 'Jake' also seems to have been the original name given to Rick Tucker – the rather carelessly prepared text refers to him as

Jake three times. According to established comic tradition, American universities have absurd names (like Astrakhan) and absurd self-advertising clothes that go with them (Tucker's jumper proclaims 'Ole Ashcan'). Even the youngest members of the faculty may be styled 'professor', and their students take unlikely combinations of subjects for their degree: Mary Lou, Tucker's wife, majors in flower-arranging and bibliography. In addition to this mild xenophobia, *The Paper Men* satirises the whole Eng. Lit. industry, wastefully devoted to discussions of ludicrous or insignificant aspects of literature: Tucker reads a paper on Barclay's relative clauses at a conference. He would sell himself or his wife for so many scraps of paper – 'letters from MacNeice, Charley Snow, Pamela, oh a whole chest full of goodies! Variant readings. The original MS of *All We Like Sheep* which differs so radically from the published version.' Golding must often have been importuned for such 'goodies' himself.

After Tucker's first disastrous encounter with Barclay at his English country house, they meet again, by Tucker's design, in Switzerland. Tucker is now married to the delectably beautiful, utterly naive Mary Lou. At one level she is a stereotype of the young American wife familiar from television situation comedy, her conversation alternately clumsy with periphrases, or simply absurd:

'He said no one else was doing you as of this moment in time.'

Or, replying to Rick's query

'Was there any sun, hon?'
'Sun, hon?'
'In our room, this afternoon, hon?'
'Why none, hon, I guess not.'

At quite another level, she is Mephistopheles' succubus,

brought to tempt the sensual Barclay to sign the pact, his Helen of Troy. Her peculiarly transparent beauty makes Barclay think of Helen, and it is as Helen that he writes of her in his journal and puts her in his next novel: 'Perhaps she didn't exist at all but was a phantom of absolute beauty like the false Helen.' Tucker appears to offer her to Barclay, but, when he touches her, her flesh is as cold and unresponsive as marble and he feels no desire to renew the contact. Rick explains more than once that Mary Lou is 'not physical', which might encourage the supposition that she is really metaphysical, and thus a phantom, although her vomiting on the floor of the bar seems physical enough. After her failure to seduce Barclay she disappears from the novel, going back to Halliday – a progress which Barclay sees as further evidence of Halliday's greed and of Tucker's extensive debts to his master; after all Mary Lou is eminently covetable. But she carries a further suggestion of a stupidity and transparency that is in no way sinister, but rather purely innocent. Such a possibility contradicts her demonic phantom role, and perhaps also Barclay's view that she is merely an element in another malicious cosmic trick against him. Although this suggestion of untouched innocence remains entirely unverifiable, it leaves her as one of the book's several mysteries.

If the temptation to fall hopelessly in love with Mary Lou seemed to Barclay yet another version of 'the clown's trousers falling down', the next episode affords him a more obvious pratfall, though it takes a second visit to the spot before he recognises this. The hotel in the Alps where he encounters the Tuckers disturbs him because he suffers from acrophobia, an irrational fear of heights, a weakness that has both a literal and a symbolic aspect. Though Barclay would like to be great, he is not prepared to pay the price, to risk the climb, and his lack of courage or self-reliance contrasts sharply with Jocelin's fearless ascent of his spire. Barclay and Rick take a walk along a mountain path shrouded in mist; as rocks tumble down close by them, Barclay leans against a rail which gives way beneath him, so that he slithers down, apparently over an infinite drop. Desperately clinging to the vertical rock face, he is gradually pulled to safety by Tucker, who hangs on to his collar, and subsequently carries him back to the hotel. Fainting with terror and furious at being rescued by the American, and thus finding himself in his debt, he resentfully mutters 'It seems I owe you my life.' His words unconsciously echo those of Jocelin to the dumb mason who saved him when the earth crept and the builders were seized with panic, and before that, the words of Caesar to Phanocles's near-silent sister, after she had removed the brass butterfly from the missile in 'Envoy Extraordinary'. Their melodramatic quality suggests that they might be some kind of private joke, deriving perhaps from one of the feebler plays Golding acted in at the outset of his career. Here their use is unconsiously ironic, since it only *seems* as if Barclay owes Tucker his life. When, some years later, he returns to the scene in bright sunlight, he realises that he was suspended only a few feet above a green meadow, a fact which Tucker must have known since he had already walked up that path on the previous day. Instead he had seized the opportunity to play the noble rescuer. For Barclay, the episode is yet another cosmic joke, this time in the form of a landscape: 'Who was it, I thought, had set about designing something theologically witty?'

The episode exposes Barclay's extreme terror, not merely of heights, but also of death. Tucker here figures as deceiver, and the phrase which Barclay irrationally associates with him, 'silence and old night' with its echoes of Milton's 'Chaos and old Night', evokes the underworld and seems to reinforce his diabolic overtones. But, like Mary Lou, Rick also reveals features that are less consistent with his role either as Mephistopheles or as a satire on American academe. As Tucker draws Barclay's attention to the two voices of the mountain stream, his own talents a listener become apparent. To listen properly is an activity that demands a self-effacing attention to the world outside the self, an ability that a man like Barclay entirely lacks, although he immediately recognises its literary potential; others, like Oliver in *The Pyramid*, who possess the ability fail to make proper use of it. Tucker, like Oliver, has a naturally good ear, the ear that made him start out by studying phonetics – it is a humanising touch. Worldly considerations have deflected him, it seems, from the one subject he really cares about. In Barclay's eyes, Tucker never fully achieves human stature, never really seems to be a man, capable of frustration, humiliation, even retaliation. But this is only a further instance of Barclay's limited powers of observation. Tucker, like the stream, also possesses a deeper, more mysterious life, whose true note cannot always be discerned beneath the high, over-anxious, sycophantic babble.

In flight from Tucker, Halliday and appeals from his wife, Barclay travels round the world, coming to rest on a Greek island. Here, as he contemplates the submarine world through snorkel and mask, he is interrupted by Johnny, an old friend from his London literary days. This encounter, occurring roughly at the centre of the book, is an important turning-point in several ways: the first half had been mainly concerned with Tucker's pursuit of Barclay, and had taken place in the everyday world; the second half is concerned with Barclay's flight not from Tucker but from God, and it constantly passes beyond the bounds of the familiar. If the first half had recorded Barclay's experiences fairly directly, experience itself now becomes confusing, evasive, hallucinatory.

The presence of Johnny, a shrewd commentator beneath his high camp mannerisms, helps the reader to recognise how far Barclay has come from any kind of normality. He is now only too evidently the victim of dislocating habits of body and mind, of drink and paranoia, as Johnny tries to warn him: 'See a priest or a shrink. If not, at least keep away from doctors acting in tandem. Otherwise they'll have you inside before you can say "dipso-schizo".' Earlier, in trying to identify what has happened to Barclay, Johnny hits on an image so apt that it remains to haunt and terrify him:

You . . . have spent your life inventing a skeleton on the outside. Like crabs and lobsters. That's terrible, you see, because the worms get inside and . . . they have the place to themselves. So my advice . . . is to get rid of the armour, the exoskeleton, the carapace, before it's too late.'

Barclay under his lobster shell, tormented by memories like worms eating into his flesh, isolated on his island, recalls *Pincher Martin*, the novel that most obviously anticipates *The Paper Men*. Both books makes use of a dreamlike or phantasmagoric narrative mode, and in both an isolated hero, clenched upon his own sinfulness and self-regard, vainly attempts to escape from a ubiquitous God. Pincher also recognised his own nature in the hard-shelled lobster; by the end he is reduced to two rigid claws, locked one upon the other, rejecting whatever lay beyond that unbearable and inescapable grip. Pincher is also haunted by the worms of memory, and in particular by the story of how the Chinese prepare a certain fish, depositing it in a tin box to be consumed by maggots, which then proceed to eat one another until only the largest and fattest cannibal-maggot is left. The story links worms not only to painful memories, to the theme of the ruthless destruction of the weaker by the stronger, but also to the barely suppressed horror of death and the decomposing body. Pincher imagines he hears the sound of the spade knocking on the tin box that contains the maggots and is also a coffin. For both Pincher and Barclay, the lobster shell signifies a determination to isolate and protect themselves from any threat to their precious egos, but Barclay's intrusive worms show up the uselessness, and worse, the positive dangers of this brittle shield. For while it cannot effectively keep the worms of memory and terror *out*, it tends instead to keep them *in*.

Both Pincher and Barclay relive some of the more degrading episodes of their past in memory, as flashbacks: each had unsuccessfully attempted to bully or blackmail a girl he desperately desired into compliance; each had made those around him serve his own ends. But for Pincher there is no time left in which to learn the lessons memory might teach. Not for him Sammy's bitter regret, Jocelin's voluntary submission to suffering and the angel's flail or Matty's deliberate atonement, each in their different way prompted by a reconsideration of the past. Pincher can only discover from his past what he unchangeably *is*; he is in a state of being, not becoming, since he is already dead when the novel begins. Barclay, although still alive and tormented by memories, also seems to have passed beyond the point of change. It seems that he cannot learn from events any more than he can rewrite the book of himself (whose composition is, in fact, dramatically interrupted by death), or reconstruct his image of the universe. He is fixed in a state of being in which even encounters with the divine seem unable to alter his nature or direction. The process of reviewing the past is potentially of great moral importance, since though we cannot alter what we have done, it may be possible to change our present selves. Memory is therefore central to the whole process of becoming something other, perhaps something better, and without the possibility of change there is little basis for optimism, either for the individual or for the race. Golding himself seems characteristically uncertain whether he regards man as a series of consecutive present moments, a sequence of 'nows', or as the outcome of what he has performed:[5]

> I think that in a sense there is nothing but the nowness of how a man feels. One side of me thinks that, and the other side of me – with thousands of years behind it – thinks that you are the sum of your good or your evil. If you have sufficient nonconformist or pagan background, you're stuck with what you are . . .

Barclay seems to be a figure who is only too patently set in the mould of what he has been.

Yet despite being past change, perhaps even paradoxically because of it, both Pincher and Barclay come under the hammer of God. From Golding's first novel, mysterious voices, the voice of the Lord of the Flies, the instructions from above or beyond, ignored or rejected at one's peril, have insistently made themselves heard, and the extensive dislocation of the narrative, both in *Pincher Martin* and *The Paper Men*, could be regarded largely as the result of the pressure of the numinous upon the action. Elsewhere individuals – Sammy, Jocelin, Matty – are confronted with the supernatural within a more conventional narrative framework, within a world more obviously governed by everyday expectations or Aristotelean probabilities. Within such a world, a reductive view of their reactions – that they are under extreme pressure and have grown 'a little crazy' – is allowed for. Such a view would miss other possibilities offered by the novels as a whole, but remains a way of licensing their testaments within texts written for a predominantly sceptical reading public. But in *Pincher Martin* and *The Paper Men* the confrontation with the supernatural breaks up the surface reality more comprehensively, emphasising the limits of probability and throwing the narrative open to larger and less finite possibilites. To some extent such confrontations are more easily integrated into looser genres – forms such as science fiction or the ghost story; they are better adapted to the greater freedoms accorded to poetry than to the technique of verisimilitude traditionally associated with the novel. It is within this technique that Golding has mainly worked, but at times – notably in these two novels – he seems deliberately to stretch it very thin or (to change the metaphor entirely) to work against its natural grain.

Pincher Martin had offered two slightly different explanations for the surreal nature of its action; the first, proposed by Pincher himself, is that alone on a rock in the Atlantic he is going slowly mad. The second, implied by the book as a whole, is that Pincher was never alone on the rock at all, but that the whole week-long ordeal was part of a struggle not to die and surrender the self that was all he had ever cared for. The action thus takes place after his death, or in the few minutes between his hitting the water and drowning. *The Paper Men* too can be read along the lines Johnny suggests, as the testament of a dipso-schizo; yet the overall effect of both these books is to confront an inescapable reality beyond man, a reality whose power is fundamentally bound up with the terror of death, the failure to love and the rejection of everything but the monstrous and furious ego. Pincher, despite all the incontrovertible evidence – 'Now there is no hope. There is nothing' – refuses to the last to recognise the place he has come to and so acknowledge defeat, but Barclay can afford to be more of a realist. Before he finally escapes from Johnny, he admits that he knows only too well where he is going:

'I'm old. I'm going faster and faster –'
'Where?'
I think I must have shouted
'Where we're all going, you bloody fool.'

In the next chapter, Barclay comes face to face with the master of that dark realm, just as Pincher had faced its black lightning.

Barclay's encounter with the God he has been fleeing from takes place on yet another island. It is Lípari, off the coast of Sicily, one of a volcanic chain, whose soil seems to consist of 'powdered pumice with knives of black glass sticking up through it'. Beneath a 'plume of black smoke like you'd get from a megaton', the earth shakes, in pointed counterpoint to Barclay's own shakes, themselves the symptoms of incipient 'delirium trimmings'. Entering the cathedral, he is confronted by a solid silver statue, striding forward with flaming red eyes, a figure that may be Christ or 'Pluto, the god of the Underworld, Hades . . . I knew in one destroying instant that all my adult life I had believed in God and this knowledge was a vision of God.' Screaming, unable to control any of his bodily functions, he falls to the ground with a fit or a stroke, and wakes to discover himself in hospital. The infernal epiphany in the cathedral shows him that he was not merely on the road to Hell, but that he had reached it – indeed had always been there, that he 'had been created by that ghastly intolerance in its own image . . . I saw I was one of the, or perhaps the only predestinate damned.' He has discovered divine justice without mercy, and in this extremity ordinary English fails him; he finds himself speaking another language that seems to be his native tongue, a language in which 'sunrise' comes out as 'liquor', 'end' as 'sin', and sin is no longer what Barclay does, but what he is. The riddle of predestination (mulled over by Marlowe's Faustus at the beginning of the play) locks itself into its familiar vicious circle, so that Barclay either cannot change because he believes himself predestined to Hell – or, because he is so predestined, cannot change. The problem is as insoluble as the question of the relationship between the individual and his theology: has the intolerance created Barclay in its own image, as he supposes, or has he projected on to the figure of Christ his own attributes? And is it possible to decide whether the power that manifests itself in the cathedral is one of good or evil? In his essay 'Belief and Creativity', Golding notes 'God works in a mysterious way,' adding 'and so, it seems, does the devil – or since that word is unfashionable I had better be democratic and call him the leader of the opposition. Sometimes the two seem to work hand in hand.'[6] Barclay warns Tucker that he cannot serve both him and Halliday – 'it's like serving God or Mammon. Guess which is which.'

Once Barclay has finally discovered where and what he is, he is filled with an acute sense of his own intolerance and lack of compassion, as well as with a bitter cynicism about the nature of freedom, a theme that has always been of the utmost importance for Golding. Just as his vision showed him only inescapable evil, so freedom confers only the right to damn oneself: 'People should be warned against it. Freedom should carry a government health warning like cancer sticks.' Up till now, Barclay's life has been characterised by his acquiescence to temptation rather than any very active pursuit of evil. Now he determines to commit a crime, and actively to further the evil of which he feels himself to be a part, or to treat another human being – in this case, Tucker – as he believes the intolerance has treated him. Ever since Johnny's advice Barclay has been conscious that in some sense Tucker is his dog, and further that if he really had a dog he would only want to kill it, partly because to do so would be to free himself from the threat implicit in its devotion, but also because to 'kill something deliberately, a dog perhaps' is a special kind of rite of passage, an active step towards commitment to the intolerance and to evil. Like Sophy when she dismissed shop-lifting as too commonplace, Barclay nevertheless rejects mere murder as 'childish stuff and unworthy of us both, unworthy of image and original. What was needed was something philosophically, or rather theologically *witty*.' Using the permission for his biography as a bait, he sets out to torment and humiliate Tucker, making him lap up wine from a saucer on the floor and insisting that if he write the biography it must also reveal the role he played in offering Mary Lou first to Barclay and then to Halliday, as mortgage for his continuing academic career. The novelist relishes this assertion of power over his victim (Tucker cannot even hit him with the saucer), watching with sadistic excitement as his victim approaches breaking point; yet even as he does so, his chest tightens as if a steel string were cutting into it, and he shudders and yells with uncontrollable fear at what he has become.

In the same essay, 'Belief and Creativity', Golding admits to guessing that 'we are in hell', while insisting that there must be other and different universes that interpenetrate our own. He continues[7]

To be in a world which is a hell, to be *of* that world and neither to believe in nor guess at anything *but* that world is not merely hell but the only possible damnation; the act of a man damning himself.

This would be an exact enough description of Barclay's spiritual condition if the novel were to end at this point, but now comes an experience that nothing else in the book so far has prepared us for, and though it seems too late to change Barclay fundamentally, it can alter his direction as well as the implications of the novel as a whole. It does so by exposing the inadequacy of his theology since he is given a glimpse of a mercy that is entirely uncovenanted, extended to the hardened sinner in the midst of his pursuit of evil, and thus casting doubt upon the 'predestinate damnation' which Barclay assumed and which his failure to change had seemed to confirm.

Returning to Rome and still searching for evidence of Halliday, his great antagonist, Barclay discovers that whatever existence Halliday may have cannot be reduced to mere print on paper: the page in *Who's Who in America* that should have contained his entry 'was bare, bare, just blank white paper'. And as he makes this discovery he sees God, or Halliday (whose name etymologically means 'Holy Day') standing on a church roof. Then follows a vision of transcendent beauty and unity of being. Its harmony of vision and sound recall Sammy's revelation on being released from his cell, and this experience too involves a symbolic liberation. The Spanish Steps become a curved instrument on which beautiful beings dance, 'and the movement was music.' He passes through a door to a dark, calm sea – 'there were creatures in the sea that sang. For the singing and the song I have no words at all.' If Hell's language is one of clumsy translations that acknowledge only the immediacy of evil, Heaven lies beyond the scope of earthly language altogether; the paper man's natural medium here reaches its terminus, and can only gesture beyond itself to silence, to the blank page, to something that cannot begin to be captured in print, something that exists beyond the human limitations of text altogether: 'since singing starts just where words leave off, where are you? Face to face with the indescribable, inexplicable, the isness, which was where you came in.'

Barclay's vision, as he later tries to explain to Liz, has the effect of reversing his whole direction: 'the boil had burst, the pain and the strain had gone.' Instead of being clenched against death, instead of fighting back against the inevitable as Pincher had done, he discovers assent. Suddenly, and apparently for the first time in his life, he is filled with a sense of irradiating happiness: 'the dream turned me round and I knew that the way I was going, towards death, was the way everybody goes, that it was – healthy, right and *consonant*.' Yet it is with the bitterest of ironies that he tries to communicate the consolation of his vision to the dying Liz, tormented by a terror of death and a horror of life that his words seem to mock at rather than to assuage. Is it another of the book's 'theologically witty' jokes that she who needed, and perhaps deserved some consolation could not find it? The comfort he offers her is as inappropriate as a sticking plaster for a severed artery. Barclay has been 'turned round', the intolerance has withdrawn, and a dawning interest in other people has been kindled in him at last, yet no deeper change is evident. His dying wife, to whom he believed himself so profoundly connected, he views dispassionately, indeed callously. Without compunction, he abandons her and goes up to town to prosecute his plans for Tucker's gradual destruction. It is already apparent (Liz has told him this in so many words) that Tucker is mad; the paper men, it seems, are bent on destroying one another. In London, at his club, Barclay warns Tucker that he plans to pre-empt his proposed biography by writing it himself. A fight in the club restaurant ensues. Barclay returns, intending to carry out his promise, only to find that his wife has died, and to learn that the stigmata he now seems to suffer from (perhaps as punishment for writing, or for sneering at that of Padre Pio) might more appropriately be associated with the crucified thieves than with the Saviour. At this point, Barclay summarises what he believes to be the main pattern of the book's events so far, rather as Talbot had done near the end of *Rites of Passage* (see above, page 129): 'Putting aside repetitions, verbals, slang, omissions, it's a fair record of the various times the clown's trousers fell down.' Barclay still regards himself as the victim of a providence whose harsh and pitiless laughter is really only another version of his own cold and mocking treatment of others. His transcendent vision has apparently born no fruit, and his stigmata are only the blackest joke of them all:

> I do think the best bit of the lot, the real, theologically witty bit of his clowning, was surely the stigmata awarded for cowardice in the face of the enemy! But St Francis and all the other suggestible creatures didn't just get it in the hands and feet, they got the wound in the side which finished off Christ or at least certified him dead. I'm missing that one; and there's hardly time or occasion for a custard pie to provide it. For I intend to disappear again . . .

Barclay intends to set out on his wanderings once more. His constant travel throughout the book seems to have been a substitute, or perhaps a compensation for his failure to progress inwardly. He makes a point of never staying anywhere long enough to allow him to discover where (sometimes literally as well as symbolically) he is or what he is. Realisations of this kind have, instead, come upon him as sudden, almost forcible revelations. As for the fatal fifth wound, which he believes that there is scarcely the time or occasion left for, the presence of Tucker in the garden, flitting from tree to tree, gun in hand, guarantees its imminence. And perhaps this is the final cosmic joke, the one that exists outside Barclay's consciousness, encouraging the view that the book as a whole ratifies his interpretation. Certainly the last scene involves an ironic reversal of the first, and not merely because this time it is Tucker who shoots Barclay in retaliation for invading what he (symbolically) regards as *his* territory. In a wider sense Barclay has succeeded in turning the tables on Tucker, retaining a grip on his own life and instead destroying, if not Tucker's soul, then at least his sanity. But Barclay has miscalculated, has underestimated his victim's spirit: the worm finally turns and turns on him; the dog bites the hand that fails to feed, the foot that has spurned. When Tucker is finally convinced that Barclay no longer intends to surrender the rights to his life, he can find no alternative but (quite literally) to take the life he believes Barclay owes him. If Barclay has become one kind of thief, Tucker becomes another. This is not so much a cosmic joke as a great reckoning, a settling of overdue debts.

But Golding is too cunning to round off the book neatly with the black theological joke that his hero in one sense did not expect and yet in another sense did. At the very last Barclay makes one last effort to free himself of the 'paper-weight of a whole life', assembling it – as poor Bounce had done – into an enormous funeral pyre of everything that he had been. Setting fire to it will not only be a symbolic act of self-purgation, it will be the very last rite of passage of all, the rite of passage that carries its subject across the boundaries of life itself. Freed of the stacked-up acts of a lifetime, he will, like Lear, 'unburden'd crawl toward death'. With no one left to mourn his departure, he intends to perform the final disappearing trick. And it seems to be the very act of preparation for this final rite that brings a softening of the sinner's heart, a relenting that one thought would never come: sud-

denly the autobiography is no longer to be used to thwart
Tucker, but will be handed over to him as a (literally)
uncovenanted mercy, a mercy such as Barclay himself received in the form of the blessed vision and such as he still
hopes for in the form of eternal annihilation of the self in
death. And suddenly the hopeful possibilities that his way
of life had repeatedly denied are asserted – not merely
happiness, which he had already found, but the change that
had continued to elude him:

> I am happy, quietly happy. How can I be happy? . . .
> Either I have broken away from the intolerance which is
> impossible, or it has let me go, which is also impossible.
> How could I change? But I have changed . . . who
> knows?

It is precisely at this moment, when the influence of the vision
finally seems to have become active, even redemptive within
him, that Tucker shoots Barclay. Is there some further and
subtler cosmic joke to be read into this that realigns the
book with divine comedy rather than with hellish farce?
Does Tucker's revenge save his victim, as Hamlet had feared
that he might save Claudius by killing him when he was at
prayer? The parable of the vineyard holds out a hope of
salvation even to those who repent at the eleventh hour, with
the promise that 'the last shall be first.' It would be the
ultimate repudiation of the Faust pattern if the Mephistophelean Tucker were finally to prove the agent of salvation
rather than damnation, if he should not seize but release the
man who had once passionately wished 'for there *not* to be
a miracle'. Barclay's final and, for him, exceptional 'Who
knows?' echoes Jocelin's 'God knows where God may be.' In
The Paper Men Golding has spun an elaborate fugue out of
some of the most ancient and unresolvable theological problems. It was scarcely to be expected that he should find easy
answers to some of the most difficult questions man has asked

himself throughout recorded history. At the end of the essay 'Belief and Creativity', Golding warned his audience that if they had 'detected contradictions and some screaming fallacies in what I have said . . . I am unrepentant . . . I claim the privilege of the storyteller; which is to be mystifying, inconsistent, impenetrable.'[8] And then, as Barclay had planned to do, Golding performed the Indian rope-trick by disappearing into his own text.

Conclusion

Considering that for most of his life William Golding has largely kept clear of literary circles and out of the public eye, a great deal is known about him. One reason for this is that at certain periods in the late 1950s and, more recently, since the publication of *Rites of Passage*, he has for his own good reasons (which in the early days included the need to make money) submitted himself patiently to ordeal by interview. Another reason is that he has published two books of occasional pieces – *The Hot Gates* and *A Moving Target* – which include lectures, commissioned articles, and autobiographical fragments that directly or indirectly reveal the man behind the novels.

Of these two main sources, his written essays are the more instructive. Like many creative writers, Golding acknowledges his own need to be a critic and an 'analyst of the process by which he gets his daily bread',[1] though he is less tolerant of efforts of others to explore his work creatively. Hence even with critics with whom he has a rapport one can sense at times when he is being interviewed a certain defensiveness, even prickliness, when they identify influences and patterns in his work to which he does not assent. This may have something to do with his past history. Golding is now so well established in the literary pantheon, his achievements recognised by the award of the Nobel prize in 1983, that it is sometimes hard to remember that his first success came at the age of 40 and his early life was regularly punctuated by the 'recurrent thud as returned manuscripts fell on the mat in the morning'. Golding attributes this initial failure to the fact that these early unpublished novels were too derivative, 'playing the sedulous ape' to other people's works.[2] One consequence of this seems to be that he now places great value on original-ity and is reluctant to agree that, for example, his work often shows the influence of Conrad, or that one of his novels shares certain characteristics with another. At interview Gol-ding often behaves like a man surprised at all the fuss, quietly insisting that critics read more into his work than is actually there.

The essays and lectures tell another story. It is often easier, in fact, to support a particular critical interpretation of a novel with evidence from essays like 'Egypt from My Inside' or 'The Ladder and the Tree' than from anything Golding has said by way of personal explication. This is because such essays reveal Golding in confessional mood, not so much trying to explain his work as attempting to understand himself and the forces which have driven him to write. As for the lectures, though one has to tread a little warily in the light of the dismissive remarks about them in the preface to *A Moving Target*, one at least – 'Belief and Creativity' – probably comes as close as we are likely to get to what Golding now believes and thus what we should expect to find reflected (even though as through a glass darkly) in his later works. It is, on the whole, encourag-ing to discover from this essay that Golding's beliefs are just as ambivalent and tentative in their conclusions as the novels themselves appear to be: 'My mind is all at sea,' he writes. 'Here is no sage to bring you a distilled wisdom. Here is an ageing novelist floundering in all the complexities of twentieth-century living, all the muddle of part beliefs.'[3] Yet from this muddle Golding manages to tease out two strands which are of central significance to him as man and novelist.

One is an unequivocal statement of how he feels the world stands and what his attitude to it now is. 'You have a right,'

he says, 'to hear what my wonder has led me . . . to guess
about the nature of things.' And that guess is by and large a
gloomy one, having apparently shifted little from the 'grief,
sheer grief, grief, grief, grief'[4] that in his view constituted the
theme of *Lord of the Flies*. Golding feels that the Lord of the
Flies, Satan, Beelzebub, the devil, or whatever he is called,
still stalks the world. His guess (dramatised as Barclay's in
The Paper Men) is that we are in Hell, but the nature of that
Hell is complicated by the fact that the devil, like God, moves
in a mysterious way: 'sometimes the two seem to work hand in
hand'; they may be difficult to distinguish. Furthermore it is
impossible to believe that the powers of darkness are in sole
control because that leaves no choice, leaves us where Barclay
was:

> To be in a world which is a hell, to be *of* that world and
> neither to believe in nor guess at anything *but* that world
> is not merely hell but the only possible damnation; the
> act of a man damning himself.

Golding believes instead that there is another signature
scribbled in the human soul – 'a sign that beyond the transient
horrors and beauties of our hell there is a Good which is
ultimate and absolute'. And this leads him to the central
statement of his own position which encompasses both the
darkness of the real world as he sees it and the certainty that,
in the totality of all things, not only seen but unseen, there is
room for hope: 'I would call myself a universal pessimist but a
cosmic optimist.'

The other clear point to emerge from this account is that
such a belief does not arise from the exercise of reason, nor
from Panglossian optimism, and certainly not from any easily
won religious consolation or promise. It springs from the
artist's experience of the creative process. That 'happening on
which the writer would bet his whole fortune, stake his whole
life as a *true* thing' occurs because writing is simply a matter of

being and defies analysis. Yet though it is a matter of being, it is not so simple to achieve. It involves an act of daring on the part of the writer, letting himself fall or perhaps deliberately diving into unknown depths which are at once within and beyond himself: 'This dive is something I have undertaken . . . on a number of occasions but I still do not know how I do it.' At certain points in the creative process the novelist experiences 'lambent moments that are his equivalent of the poet's lyrical impulse', times when 'he knows he is on to something good' and fears interruption from a man from Porlock hammering on the door. Golding rejects the idea that these 'moments of genuine creativity' are merely self-induced, merely imagination rearranging the material of the mind:

> My hope is better. The writer watches the greatest mystery of all. It is the moment of vital awareness, the moment of most passionate and *unsupported* conviction. It shines or cries . . . Like God, he looks on his creation and knows what he has done.

In a sense, all this sounds remarkably close to the conventional romantic position and it is not surprising to find the interruption of the man from Porlock coming to his mind so readily when Golding is talking about the 'memories of moments of absolute conviction' that are central to the creative act. Yet though Coleridge also sought for moments of conviction and regarded them as essentially creative, the differences between his view and Golding's are as striking as the similarities. Golding, though deeply religious, is not a believer in a conventional sense, nor does he follow Shelley in subscribing to a literary creed that might provide a substitute for belief. He is a guesser who would like his epitaph to read 'He wondered', who 'suffers the varying levels or intensities of belief' which are part of the human condition. He has no fixed centre, and this accounts for the very varied atmospheres, tones and attitudes present in his work – sometimes deeply

pessimistic as in *The Pyramid* and, perhaps, *Rites of Passage* and
sometimes, as in *The Spire* and *Darkness Visible*, illuminated by
the possibility of a faith that derives from the memories of
those moments of passionate conviction that convince him
that something is better than nothing, good than evil, love
than hatred or indifference.

Golding's sense of the importance of these moments of
conviction, and of their consequence for his beliefs more generally, has been reflected in his increasing concern with the
role and nature of the artist as the chief recipient of such
moments. This concern first became apparent in *Free Fall* and
has been markedly present ever since. Though he has said
directly, as well as through the fiction of *The Paper Men*, that he
distrusts the age's worship of the artist, Golding is sufficiently
a child of his age, or perhaps of the romantic movement,[5]
to perceive a vital connection betwen the presence of a mysterious beauty or coherence in the universe and the artist's
apprehension of it, and further, the communication of that
apprehension to a wider audience. Over and over again, the
later novels approach the question of the artist's vision, from
one angle or another: in *The Spire*, there is Jocelin's 'folly',
sustained by faith and stained by sacrifice; in *The Pyramid*
there is the music which the main characters vainly strive to
make, and which Oliver betrays for more worldly considerations. *Darkness Visible* splits the creative process between the
cold and evil plot-making of Sophy and the passionate insights
of the ignorant and visionary Matty, and there is a different
but comparable duality in *Rites of Passage* where the sociable,
rational Talbot confronts the isolated, inspired Colley. *The
Paper Men* is the novel most directly concerned with the
relationship of the writer to the modern world, as well as with
the inextricably complex relationship of creativity and belief.
Its novelist, Barclay, deflected by self-absorption from finer
perceptions, creates a harsh god in his own image, yet conviction and beauty finally coincide for him in a moment of unique
revelation. Such moments are not, however, the sole preroga-

tive of the artist, but are more universal, though it is the artist's special privilege to recreate them. The artist takes the ordinary world and transforms it even as such moments transform the ordinary world, setting it suddenly alight:

> On any of us the moment may strike, the awareness of something not argued over but directly apprehended, perception that the sun makes music as of old. As we pause, like Leopold Bloom after that long Odyssey of a single day, we may look up and be pierced by the sight of the heaven tree hung with humid night blue fruit. Music may present us with its passing ineffable proposition. We may stare through a rectangle of canvas into a magically perfect world and get a touch of paradise.

Notes

The epigraph is taken from Craig Raine's interview with Golding, part of his programme *Cabin'd, Cribb'd, Confine'd*, broadcast on 23 December 1983.

Abbreviations have been used for Golding's two books of essays, HG for *The Hot Gates* (1965) and MT for *A Moving Target* (1982).

Introduction

1. 'A Moving Target', MT, p. 166.
2. Reprinted as 'Fable', HG, p. 100.
3. See Virginia Tiger, *William Golding – The Dark Fields of Discovery* (1974), p. 142.
4. Interview with James Baker, *Twentieth Century Literature* (Summer 1982, vol. 28, no. 2), p. 145.
5. 'Fable', HG, p. 99.
6. In 'The Parting of the Ways', two radio talks broadcast on 28 June and 3 July 1959; reprinted in *The Listener*, 16 July and 30 July 1959.
7. In a letter to Don Crompton, but Golding has made the same point in interviews with W.L. Webb (see below, chapter 2, note 10) and John Haffenden (see below chapter 5, note 4).
8. 'Egypt from My Inside', HG, pp. 79, 80, 81.
9. 'The Ladder and the Tree', HG, pp. 172-3, 174.
10. Interview with Frank Kermode, broadcast on 28 August 1959 and partly reprinted in *Books and Bookmen* (October 1959), p. 10.

11. 'Egypt from My Inside'.
12. 'Belief and Creativity', MT, p. 198.
13. 'A Moving Target', MT, p. 198.
14. Ibid., p. 168.
15. Interview with James Baker, *Twentieth Century Literature*, p. 161.
16. Ibid., p. 158.
17. 'Rough Magic', MT, pp. 143, 145.
18. 'Intimate Relations', MT, p. 124.
19. MT, pp. 164-6.
20. 'Belief and Creativity', MT, p. 199.

Chapter 1   *The Spire*

1. MT, p. 10.
2. See 'Digging for Pictures', HG, p. 61.
3. HG, especially pp. 166, 170.
4. Golding has said 'I put a Cold Harbour in *The Spire* to render the whole concept critic-proof.' See Virginia Tiger, *William Golding*, p. 192.
5. 'A Moving Target', MT, p. 167.

Chapter 2   *The Pyramid*

1. 'Rough Magic', MT, pp. 145-6.
2. Quoted by Virginia Tiger, *William Golding*, p. 214.
3. HG, p. 166.
4. HG, p. 159.
5. HG, pp. 145-6.
6. HG, p. 161.
7. 'Egypt from My Inside', HG, p. 71.
8. Interview with James Baker, *Twentieth Century Literature*, p. 154.
9. Ibid., p. 153.
10. *Guardian*, 11 October 1980, p. 12.
11. Interview with James Baker, *Twentieth Century Literature*, p. 154.
12. Ibid., p. 153.
13. Ibid., p. 158.

Chapter 3 *The Scorpion God*

1. 'Before the Beginning', Golding's review of Grahame Clark's *World Prehistory* in *The Spectator*, 26 May 1961, p. 768.
2. Interview with James Baker, *Twentieth Century Literature*, p. 158.
3. Discussed in interview with Frank Kermode, 28 August 1959, and developed in the essay 'Fable', HG, pp. 85-6.
4. HG, pp. 71-2 and MT, p. 44-5. The quotations that follow are all from that essay.
5. See Walter B. Emery, *Archaic Egypt* (1961; latest edition, Penguin, 1984), p. 32. This has been my main source for what follows. Emery discusses and illustrates the mace-head, pp. 42-3.
6. Interview with James Baker, *Twentieth Century Literature*, p. 158.
7. See Walter B. Emery, *Archaic Egypt*, p. 108.
8. HG, especially pp. 67-70.
9. Interview with James Baker, *Twentieth Century Literature*, p. 158. See also Herodotus's *The Histories*, translated Aubrey de Selincourt (1954, revised by A. R. Burn and reprinted for Penguin, 1972), p. 142. Herodotus on the High Priest, p. 144; on the priests' cleanliness, p. 143.
10. On the mace-head see note 5 above; also W. Stevenson Smith, *The Art and Architecture of Ancient Egypt* (1958, revised by W. Kelly Simpson and reprinted for Penguin, 1981), p. 33-4. Golding understandably confused the mace-head with the schist palette representing Narmer in his interview with James Baker, *Twentieth Century Literature*, p. 160.
11. Herodotus, *The Histories*, p. 165.
12. Ibid., pp. 136-7.
13. 'Egypt from My Inside', HG, p. 81.
14. Interview with James Baker, *Twentieth Century Literature*, p. 160.
15. Ibid., p. 159.
16. 'Billy the Kid', HG, pp. 162-3.

Chapter 4 *Darkness Visible*

1. See above, Introduction, note 7.

2. Charles Monteith, Golding's publisher, described *Lord of the Flies* as he first saw it in Raine's radio programme *Cabin'd, Cribb'd, Confin'd* (for details, see note on epigraph above).

3. Matty's old Bible with wooden covers which he found in Australia may also act as a kind of talisman for him. If so, this might explain why the spirits later test his obedience by making him throw it away, thus requiring him to trust himself entirely to their protection.

4. Craig Raine enlarged tellingly on this point and others in his review of *Darkness Visible* in the *New Statesman*, 12 October 1979, pp. 552-3.

Chapter 5   *Rites of Passage*

1. Interview with James Baker, *Twentieth Century Literature*, p. 132. See also Elizabeth Longford's *Wellington*, vol. I, *The Years of the Sword* (1969), p. 51.

2. 'Belief and Creativity', MT, p. 199.

3. Interview with James Baker, *Twentieth Century Literature*, p. 164.

4. Interview with John Haffenden, in *Quarto* (November 1980), p. 11.

5. Interview with James Baker, *Twentieth Century Literature*, p. 161.

6. Ibid., p. 163, and interview with W.L. Webb in the *Guardian*, 11 October 1980, p. 12.

7. Interview with James Baker, *Twentieth Century Literature*, p. 161.

8. HG, p. 135.

9. In *The Sunday Times*, 19 October 1980, p. 42.

10. Interview with John Haffenden, in *Quarto*, p. 9.

Chapter 6   *The Paper Men*

1. A characteristically sympathetic account of the book was given by Frank Kermode in *The London Review of Books* (1 March 1984, vol. 6, no. 4), pp. 15-6, to which I am indebted.

2. 'Belief and Creativity', MT p. 185.

3. 'Rough Magic', MT, p. 144. In 'My First Book' (MT, p. 152)

Golding described his own experience of being hypnotised as a young man.

4. A habit he shares with his creator: 'I keep everything I have scribbled on; there's masses and masses of it' Golding told Victoria Glendinning in an interview for *The Sunday Times*, 19 October 1980, p. 39.

5. Interview with John Haffenden, in *Quarto*, p. 10.

6. MT, p. 198.

7. MT, p. 201.

8. MT, p. 202.

Conclusion

1. 'A Moving Target', MT, p. 155.

2. Ibid., pp. 160-2.

3. 'Belief and Creativity', MT, p. 192. Hereafter all quotations are taken from that essay, unless otherwise stated.

4. 'A Moving Target', MT, p. 163.

5. Ibid., p. 155.

Index

First published 1985

Basil Blackwell Publisher Ltd
108 Cowley Road, Oxford OX4 1JF, UK

Basil Blackwell Inc.
432 Park Avenue South, Suite 1505,
New York, NY 10016, USA

British Library Cataloguing in Publication Data

Crompton, Don
A view from the spire: William Golding's later novels.
1. Golding, William——Criticism and Interpretation
I. Title   II. Briggs, Julia
823'.914   PR6013.035Z/

ISBN 0-631-13826-9

Library of Congress Cataloging in Publication Data

Crompton, Don.
A view from the spire.

Includes bibliographical references and index.
1. Golding, William, 1911-   --Criticism and interpretation.
I. Briggs, Julia.   II. Title.
PR6013.035Z597   1984   823'.914   84-16742
ISBN 0-631-13826-9

Typeset by Dentset, Waterstock, Oxford OX9 1JT
Printed in Great Britain by Billing and Sons Ltd, Worcester

A VIEW
FROM THE SPIRE

William Golding's Later Novels

Don Crompton

Edited and completed by
Julia Briggs

Basil Blackwell